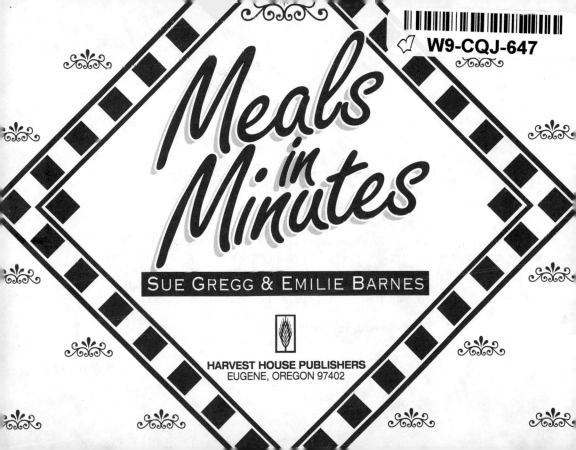

Meals in Minutes

Sue Gregg & Emilie Barnes

HARVEST HOUSE PUBLISHERS
EUGENE, OREGON 97402

Meals in Minutes

Emilie Barnes challenged me to consider the *Meals in Minutes* concept when she heard the story of Carol. Carol purchased my *Main Dishes* cookbook, then prepared and froze 18 casseroles. A neighbor heard about the ready-to-serve resources in Carol's freezer and persuaded her to sell one because she desperately needed a main dish for her next meal. That launched Carol into a small business of selling casseroles to her neighbors and friends.

That encouragement prompted me to write *Casseroles for Busy Women*, with 26 recipes for freezing along with shopping and assembly lists and menus. With *Meals in Minutes*, I have taken the idea a step further and added nonfreezer quick meals as well.

While the focus is on convenience, nutritional value is not neglected. How nutritious are *Meals in Minutes*? Let me compare our "nutrition score" with typical American dinners: Our meals average 41% lower in fat, 40% lower in cholesterol, 41% lower in sodium, and 221% higher in dietary fiber. And to top it off, they cost less! How is that possible? Because I use less meat and dairy products and add whole grains and other quality ingredients. Vegetarian alternatives can cut costs further, along with the fat and calories.

My dream is that *Meals in Minutes* will pass your taste test and help you achieve Emilie's goal of giving you "More Hours in *Your* Day!"

Sue Gregg

ALSO BY SUE GREGG AND EMILIE BARNES

Eating Right! A Realistic Approach to a Healthy Lifestyle (Harvest House)

Eating Better with Sue, Video (Fabian Productions)
    Eating Better with Sue Cooking Course Guide
    Eating Better with Sue Cooking Course Leader's Guide

SUE GREGG (Eating Better Cookbooks)
    Main Dishes
    Casseroles
    Soups & Muffins
    Lunches & Snacks
    More Than Breakfasts
    Desserts
    Holiday Menus
    The Creative Recipe Organizer
    The Eating Better Menu Planner
    Quantity Recipes

EMILIE BARNES (Harvest House)
    More Hours in My Day
    Survival for Busy Women
    The Creative Home Organizer
    The 15 Minute Organizer
    The Holiday Organizer
    Growing a Great Marriage
    Things Happen When Women Care
    The Daily Planner
    The Spirit of Loveliness
    The 15 Minute Money Manager

CONTENTS

This Cookbook Is About...

1. CONVENIENCE

2. APPETITE APPEAL

3. NUTRITIONAL VALUE

4. COST CONTROL

1. Convenience

3-IN-1 FREEZER MEALS

•

CROCKPOT AND QUICK MEALS

•

PLAN AHEAD • DO AHEAD
MENUS, SHOPPING, BAKING

3-in-1 Cooking

PLAN #1 • Prepare 3 main dish recipes at once. • Eat 1. • Freeze 2.	**PLAN #3** • Singles: Prepare 1 recipe and divide in 3. • Eat 1. • Freeze 2.
PLAN #2 • Prepare 1 recipe. • Multiply to serve 3 meals. • Eat 1.• Freeze 2.	**PLAN #4** • Prepare 3 freezer sets at once.

Menus Planned

WITH

FORTY-SEVEN MAIN DISHES

SEVEN EASY SALADS

SEVEN POPULAR VEGETABLES

SEVEN DELICIOUS BREADS

SEVEN OCCASIONAL DESSERTS

2.
Appetite Appeal

Keys to Taste and Nutrition

- Use quality ingredients.

- Include all food groups.

- Make fish, poultry, meat, dairy
  S-T-R-E-T-C-H.

- Provide vegetarian and allergy alternatives.

- Include lots of vegetables, fresh and frozen.

- Liberally use whole grains and legumes.

- Use fresh fruits moderately.

"Everything is permissible for me"—but not everything is beneficial (1 Corinthians 6:12).

3. Nutritional Value

(See p. xv for Nutrient Data Sources.)

GET PLENTY OF THESE

	AMERICAN DAILY AVERAGE *(for all meals)*	**RECOMMENDED DAILY AVERAGE** *(for all meals)*	**MEALS IN MINUTES DINNER MENU AVERAGE** *(for main meal only)*
COMPLEX CARBOHYDRATE	22%*	55-65%	58-59%
DIETARY FIBER	7-14 grams	25-40 grams	20 grams

Percentages listed are % of total calories.

*1981 Levels

I have set before you life and death, blessings and curses. Now choose life, so that you and your children may live and that you may love the LORD your God, listen to his voice, and hold fast to him (Deuteronomy 30:19-20).

LIMIT THESE

	AMERICAN DAILY AVERAGE *(for all meals)*	**RECOMMENDED DAILY AVERAGE** *(for all meals)*	**MEALS IN MINUTES DINNER MENU AVERAGE** *(for main meal only)*
PROTEIN	12%* (high animal)	10-15% (more vegetable)	15-16% (more vegetable)
TOTAL FAT	38-42%	30%	26%
Saturated	16%*	10%	8-9%
Monounsaturated	19%*	10%	10-11%
Polyunsaturated	7%*	10%	8-9%
CHOLESTEROL	450-500 mg.	250-300 mg.	90-93 mg.
SODIUM	4,000-6,000 mg.	1,100-3,300 mg.	876-924 mg.
SUGAR	2/3 cup (126 lbs./year)	11 tsp. honey or 6.5 tbsp. sugar	1-2 tsp. without desserts

Percentages listed are % of total calories.

*1981 Levels

Nutrient data for this book has been compiled from *Sue's Nutridata* computer program based on the following sources (listed in order of first use where data is available):

Total Nutrition Guide by Jean Carper (Bantam Books, 1989).

Food Values of Portions Commonly Used by Jean A. T. Pennington and Helen Nichols Church (Harper & Row Publishers, 1985).

Nutrition Wizard, computer data program by Michael Jacobson (CSPI, 1986).

Nutrition Almanac, Revised Edition by Nutrition Search, Inc., John D. Kirschmann, director (McGraw-Hill Book Company, 1979).

Laurel's Kitchen by Laurel Robertson, Carol Flinders, and Bronwen Godfrey (Nilgiri Press, 1976).

Selected food package labels.

Exchanges reflect values used by the American Diabetes Association, Inc. and Weight Watchers.

All data has been rounded off to the nearest half or whole, exchange values to the nearest fourth. Data is based on first listed ingredient choice unless specified otherwise.

4. Cost Control

- Meals average $1.70 per person.
(Cost provided with every recipe and menu!)

- Comparable to USDA estimates for
low- to moderate-cost home food plans.

- Save $$ with meatless and meat-dairy
stretcher meals.

- Average 52 lbs. meat and poultry per person per year
(as compared to the American average of 176 lbs.).

Why spend money on what is not bread,
and your labor on what does not satisfy?
Listen, listen to me, and eat what is good,
and your soul will delight in the richest of fare.

ISAIAH 55:2

BASIC STOCK LIST

Ingredients and food items frequently used in recipes and menus that may be stored longer than 1 week. An asterisk (*) indicates item of recommended nutritional quality may be available only in health food stores. See page references for more buying information.

DAIRY (p. 72)
butter, unsalted (for freezer) (p. 6)
cheddar cheese
Parmesan cheese
sour cream
tofu (p. 82)
yogurt

DRIED FRUIT/NUTS (p. 146)
almonds, whole or slivered
coconut, unsweetened*
raisins
walnuts

FISH/POULTRY
tuna, canned in water (p. 30)
salmon, canned (p. 30)
ground turkey (for freezer) (p. 42)
chicken (for freezer) (p. 62)
franks* (for freezer) (p. 82)

Continued on p. 3.

FLOURS (or grain for milling flour)
cornmeal* (p. 177)
whole wheat pastry flour* (p. 163)
Kamut* and/or spelt,* optional (p. 163)
wheat bran (p. 168)

GRAINS/BEANS
brown and/or converted rice (p. 40)
dry beans (legumes) (p. 146):
    black beans (turtle beans)
    black-eyed peas
    lentils
    navy beans
    pinto
    split peas
corn chips* (p. 177)
pastas* (p. 20):
    macaroni
    noodles
    spaghetti

FROZEN FOODS
orange juice, frozen, 6 oz.
vegetables:
    corn
    green beans
    peas

PRODUCE
carrots
celery
garlic cloves
onions
parsley (p. 54)
potatoes

CONDIMENTS (p. 94)
mayonnaise
mustard
pickle relish
jam

Ingredients and food items frequently used in recipes and menus that may be stored longer than 1 week. An asterisk (*) indicates item of recommended nutritional quality may be available only in health food stores. See page references for more buying information.

BAKING/COOKING SUPPLIES
apple cider vinegar
baking powder* (p. 163)
baking soda
buttermilk, powdered (p. 172)
carob powder (p. 190)
chicken broth (p. 62)
chocolate, unsweetened, optional
cocoa powder, optional
cornstarch
crystalline fructose (p. 163)
honey
ketchup* (p. 94)
lemon juice
olive/canola/safflower oil (p. 171)
salt* (p. 163)
Sue's Kitchen Magic (p. 52)
soy sauce (p. 94)
vanilla extract
Worcestershire sauce* (p. 94)

BREADS, WHOLE GRAIN* (for freezer) (p. 164)
buns (hamburger/hot dog) (p. 74)
dinner rolls
sandwich slice bread
sourdough bread
tortillas (p. 177)

CANNED GOODS
green chilies, diced
mushrooms, stems and pieces, optional
pineapple, unsweetened
ripe olives, sliced
spaghetti/pasta sauce,* optional (p. 94)
tomato paste (p. 94)
tomato sauce (p. 94)
tomatoes, whole, pieces, stewed (p. 94)
water chestnuts, sliced

HERBS AND SPICES (listed, p. 5)

Continued on p. 2.

3

1. Arrange smaller spices and herbs alphabetically. Number them consecutively with plastic tape. Jars and cans do not need to be same shape or size.

2. Place on turntables. Place larger containers in the middle.

3. Quickly locate any item alphabetically and return it by the number.

4. Plastic tape can easily be removed from empty to new containers.

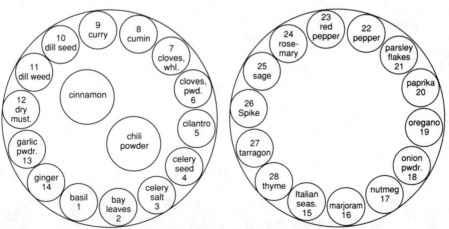

4

This list includes herbs and spices for all recipes in this book, and then some for most other recipe needs.

allspice
basil leaves, dried
bay leaves
celery salt
celery seed
chili powder
cilantro (coriander leaf)
cinnamon
cinnamon sticks
cloves, powdered
cloves, whole
cumin powder
curry powder
dill seed
dill weed
dry mustard
garlic powder
ginger, powdered

Italian seasoning
lemon peel, dried
marjoram leaves, dried
nutmeg
onion powder
orange peel, dried
oregano leaves, dried
paprika
parsley flakes
pepper (black)
poppy seeds
red pepper (cayenne)
rosemary leaves, dried
sage
Spike seasoning *(health food store)*
tarragon leaves, dried
thyme leaves, dried
turmeric

KEY: RT—Room Temperature; R—Refrigerator; F—Freezer
Store all foods in tightly covered containers in dark, dry, cool place.

BROWN RICE: RT—1 month; R or F—6 months.

GRAINS: RT—1 year (storing in freezer protects from infestation). If mild infestation occurs, place in freezer for 3 days, then sift critters out through a colander. (For whole grain flours, see p. 165.)

HERBS AND SPICES, DRIED: RT—6-12 months; keep away from all appliances that give off heat.

LEGUMES (DRY BEANS): RT—1 year (beans toughen over time, requiring more cooking).

NUTS AND SEEDS, SHELLED: Most: RT—2-3 months; R—6 months; F—1 Year.

PASTAS: RT—1 month; R or F—2-4 months.

UNSALTED BUTTER: F—6-9 months. If used only occasionally for cooking or baking, keep in the freezer. Unsalted butter turns rancid more quickly than salted butter.

OILS: olive oil, RT—4-12 months (satisfactory under 76-80°); R—6-12 months. Others, R—4 months (always refrigerate oils without preservatives, except olive oil).

PLANS FOR FREEZING

There are a variety of systems for freezing meals. Four plans are listed on p. ix. Increase any recipe as desired. Combine freezer sets to make more than 3 dishes at one time. Our freezer sets are designed for flexibility as well as simplicity.

COOKING FOODS FOR THE FREEZER

Since reheated frozen dishes tend to get cooked more, cook vegetables until just crisp-tender and pastas *al dente* (pp. 152-153). You may wish to withhold vegetables that give high color to the dish and add just before serving (green pepper, for example). Since herbs tend to weaken when frozen, you may wish to add them to thawed dishes. Ingredients that do not freeze well have not been used in our freezer recipes.

THE FREEZER

For top flavor quality and retained nutrient value, meals should be frozen rapidly. This will be facilitated by the following:

1. Cool especially hot dishes in the refrigerator before freezing.
2. Do not fill more than 10% of the freezer space with unfrozen dishes or foods.
3. Maintain the freezer temperature at 0° F.

Eight weeks is about the maximum for a frozen prepared meal to retain its quality of flavor and texture. Plan to use it within 3 to 6 weeks.

CONVENTIONAL METHOD

Run hot water over top, sides, and bottom of container until contents snap out easily. Place in baking pan or casserole dish lightly sprayed with non-stick spray. Cover. Thaw in refrigerator about 24 hours (not at room temperature!) and reheat in preheated oven (generally 350°) until hot through—about 20 to 30 minutes. To reheat unthawed, allow about 1½ to 2 hours for a 2-quart casserole, or 1½ to 3 times longer than needed to heat if thawed. To heat in saucepan on range top, cover and keep the heat very low. Saucy dishes thickened with flour can separate during freezing. Stir when thawed and again while reheating.

MICROWAVE METHOD

Follow same procedure as above for loosening the lid. Most average family-sized casseroles require about 30 to 60 minutes on defrost setting and about 5 to 10 minutes at full power to reheat. See *Using the Microwave*, p. 10.

Any variations for thawing and reheating are given with specific recipes.

INVEST IN QUALITY

Invest in an adequate supply of quality freezer containers with secure lids that will not chip or crack easily. Plastic is ideal for freezing. Two excellent brands are *Superseal Microwave Store 'n Serve* and *Rubbermaid*. If planning to microwave-thaw and reheat, get containers suitable for both microwaving and freezer storage, allowing the use of one container from start to finish.

FOR CONVENTIONAL THAWING AND REHEATING

Use freezer containers similar in size and shape to your conventional baking pans and casserole dishes. Make the dish, freeze it in freezer container (no foil wrapping or packaging to fuss with or repeatedly spend money on). To thaw and reheat, transfer the contents of the frozen container to the baking pan or casserole of similar size (see p. 8). In this way, while you may have several freezer containers of similar size, you only need 1 conventional baking pan or casserole of the same size. For freezing sauces and soups to be heated on top of the range, I use saved plastic quart yogurt containers or *Tupperware*. For a few dishes that are oven-baked before freezing, it is convenient to freeze them in the same oven-proof baking dish. After these are frozen they may be transferred to another container or wrapped in plastic wrap, then foil, if desired. Any variations for freezing are given with specific recipes.

I want to offer alternatives not only for improved nutrition, but for convenience as well. The microwave has been the revolutionary convenience appliance of our time, so I am reluctant to caution you about its use. However, preliminary research studies suggest that microwave cooking may be cause for concern in at least three areas:

1. Possible cancer-causing and cholesterol-raising effects
2. Negative effects on the nutritive value of foods
3. Possible effects of direct microwave oven radiation emissions

Even though the microwave option for thawing and reheating is included here, in my home I use conventional methods. In the recipes, all the preliminary cooking is done conventionally.

An attractive alternative to the microwave is the turbo convection oven. Compact in size, it takes up less space than a microwave. Home convection ovens circulate air heated by an electrical coil with a fan. They thaw frozen foods quickly, use about 60% less energy, and can cook in less than half the time of a conventional oven. They cost from $100 to $300 and are available in many department and discount stores.

FREEZER SET #1
• *Sweet 'n Sour Beans, p. 15* • *Chicken Curry, p. 17* • *Tuna Fettucini, p. 19*

MEATS/FISH/POULTRY:
ground turkey, 1 lb.
chicken, 1-1½ lbs. boneless breast
tuna fish, 6.5 oz. can

DAIRY:
butter, ½ stick (¼ C.), optional
sour cream, ½ pt. (1 C.)
Parmesan cheese, 2 oz. (½ C.)

FRESH PRODUCE:
onions, 3 medium
celery, 5 ribs
apple, 1 tart green

FROZEN:
frozen peas, 3 oz. (½ C.)

GRAINS/BEANS/PASTAS/NUTS:
*whole grain noodles, 8 oz.
*whole wheat pastry flour, ½ C.
*chicken broth, 24 oz.
 butter beans, 2—15 oz. cans
 green lima beans, 2—17 oz. cans
 kidney beans, 2—15½ oz. cans
 vegetarian beans in tomato sauce
   (*Heinz*), 2—1 lb. cans or baked beans
   if not available
almonds, 2 oz. (¼ C.), whole or slivered

STAPLES:
Check for honey, molasses, ketchup, soy
sauce, vinegar, Worcestershire sauce, lemon
juice.

SEASONINGS/HERBS:
Check *Herb and Spice Cupboard* (p. 5)
against recipes.

*It may be necessary to purchase these items at a health food store.

Total calories, fat %, and estimated cost of each menu are based on these serving sizes unless otherwise stated in the menu box. If more than one choice is given, data is based on first listed. Food cost is based on 1992 average food prices and is rounded off to the nearest $.05 upward for all menus and most of the recipes. See p. xv for nutrient data sources.

MENU

**624 Calories
27% Fat
$1.20**

MAIN DISH	recipe serving size
RICE, POTATOES, PASTA	¾ C. rice 6 oz. potato 1 C. pasta
VEGETABLE	¾ C.
SALAD	2 C. tossed; ¾ C. other types 1 serving gelatin average serving of arranged salad
SALAD DRESSING	1 tbsp. oil or fat based; 2 tbsp. lowfat type
BREAD	1½ pieces or recipe serving size
SPREAD	1½ tsp. butter or butter spread 1 tbsp. jam or other spread
FRUIT OR DESSERT	1 piece fruit or average serving of a variety fruit plate, or recipe serving size

ASSEMBLY TIPS

- **SWEET 'N SOUR BEANS,** *p. 15*
  - **CHICKEN CURRY,** *p. 17*
  - **TUNA FETTUCINI,** *p. 19*

1. Assemble ingredients for recipes on trays. Get out: 1 large fry pan, large pan to cook pasta, pan to cook chicken, 1 small and 1 large mixing bowl, freezer containers.

2. Use the same fry pan to cook turkey and onions, cook curry sauce, assemble fettucini ingredients, washing pan out as needed.

3. For curry, start cooking chicken or have it cooked in advance with broth (p. 145). Start heating water for noodles and browning of ground turkey while chopping fresh ingredients.

4. Prepare fresh vegetables at the same time:
   - Slice 2 onions for *Sweet 'n Sour Beans.*
   - Chop 1 onion for curry and fettucini, using ¼ C. for fettucini.
   - Chop 1½ C. celery for curry and fettucini.
   - Chop ¼ C. almonds (if using whole).
   - Chop apple for curry (unpeeled preferred).

5. Complete each dish in order: beans, curry, fettucini.

6. Place in freezer containers, label, cool in refrigerator if needed, freeze. Include recipe page # on label to refer back to later.

13

❧❦ SWEET 'N SOUR BEANS ❦❧

To thaw and reheat, see p. 8.

1 C. serving, using 90% fat-free ground turkey (approx. $.85)
Exchanges: 1.75 meat, 2.5 bread, 0.5 vegetable
299 calories
18 grams protein (24%)
3 grams fat (10%), 22 mg. cholesterol
49.5 grams carbohydrate (66%), 10.5 grams dietary fiber
1,118 mg. sodium (reduce 40% by thoroughly rinsing beans 1 minute under running water)

MENU

635 Calories
20% Fat
$1.55*

SWEET 'N SOUR BEANS *(p. 15)*

TOSSED SALAD *(p. 158)*
WITH SWEET LITE DRESSING *(p. 160)*

CORNBREAD *(p. 178)*
WITH HONEY BUTTER SPREAD *(p. 173)*

For size servings on which data is based, see p. 12. To adjust fat level of menus, see p. 193.

❦ SWEET 'N SOUR BEANS ❦

Absolutely yummy. Low-low fat even with ground turkey!

1. Blend turkey with seasonings; brown; remove from pan:

1 lb. ground turkey *(p. 42)*	**¹/₂ tsp. sage**
1 tsp. salt	**¹/₂ tsp. thyme**
¹/₂ tsp. nutmeg	**¹/₁₆ tsp. cayenne pepper**

2. Add onions to the pan with a little water; cover and cook until tender. Add, cover, and simmer for 20 minutes:

2 medium onions, sliced, separated into rings	**1 tsp. mustard** *(p. 94)*
¹/₃ C. apple cider vinegar	**1 tsp. salt**
¹/₄ C. honey	**¹/₂ tsp. garlic powder**

3. Drain and rinse first 3 beans. Combine beans with onion mixture and turkey in a large bowl:

2—15 oz. cans butter beans	**2—16 oz. cans *Heinz Vegetarian Beans in Tomato Sauce* (if not available, use baked beans)**
2—15¹/₂ oz. cans red kidney beans	
2—17 oz. cans green lima beans (if not available, use 16 oz. frozen)	

4. Blend together and mix in thoroughly:

¹/₄ C. molasses (blackstrap preferred)	**1 tsp. Worcestershire sauce** *(p. 94)*
¹/₄ C. ketchup *(p. 94)*	

VEGETARIAN ALTERNATIVE: Omit ground turkey (reduces quantity by 2 C.).

CHICKEN CURRY

To thaw and reheat, see p. 8.

Per serving of 6—about 1 C., *using 3 C. chicken, Spike seasoning not included*
(approx. $1.40)

   Exchanges: 3 meat, 1.75 fat, 0.5 bread, 0.25 fruit, 0.75 vegetable
   333 calories
   35.5 grams protein (43%)
   13.5 grams fat (36%), 87 mg. cholesterol
   17.5 grams carbohydrate (21%), 4 grams dietary fiber
   268 mg. sodium

MENU

694 Calories
20% Fat
$2.10*

CHICKEN CURRY *(p. 17)*

BROWN RICE *(p. 148)*

FROZEN OR FRESH PEAS

ARRANGED ORANGE / PINEAPPLE SALAD *(p. 158)*
WITH SWEET MAYONNAISE DRESSING *(p. 160)*

*For size servings on which data is based, see p. 12. To adjust fat level of menus, see p. 193.

5-6 Cups ~ Serves 4-6

One of our favorite meals! Serve over Brown Rice (p. 148 or 150).

1. In fry pan over moderate heat, cook onion, celery, and apple in butter or oil until barely tender, about 10 minutes:

    ¹/₄ C. olive oil *(p. 171)* **or unsalted butter, melted**
    1 small onion, slivered or cut in thin rings (separate rings)
    4 medium ribs celery, thinly sliced on diagonal
    1 tart green apple (about 1 C.), unpeeled, chopped

2. Mix in flour; stir constantly about 1 minute. Remove from heat and blend in chicken broth and seasonings:

    ¹/₂ C. whole wheat pastry flour *(p. 163)*   **¹/₄ teaspoon garlic powder**
        (or 6 tbsp. unbleached flour)   **¹/₂ tsp. soy sauce** *(p. 94)*
    3 C. chicken broth *(p. 62 or 145)*   **3 tsp. curry powder, to taste**
    1 tsp. salt (less with salted broth)   **1 tsp. Spike seasoning, optional** *(p. 5)*
    ¹/₂ tsp. paprika

3. Return to moderate heat to cook, stirring constantly, until thickened; gently stir in chicken (do not over-stir):

    2-3 C. cooked boneless chicken breast, cut in small chunks *(p. 145)*

VEGETARIAN ALTERNATIVE: Omit broth and chicken. Add **3 C. water** plus **1 tbsp.** ***Sue's Kitchen Magic* seasoning** *(p. 52)* and **1 C. cashews** (roasted, unsalted).

TUNA FETTUCINI

To thaw and reheat, see p. 8

1 serving of 6, using light sour cream (approx. $.85)
    Exchanges: 1.25 meat, 3.75 fat, 2 bread
    384 calories
    20 grams protein (21%)
    19 grams fat (45%), 58 mg. cholesterol
    33 grams carbohydrate (34%), 9 grams dietary fiber
    57 mg. sodium

MENU

TUNA FETTUCINI *(p. 19)*

FANTASTIC BROCCOLI *(p. 156)*

ARRANGED TOMATO/CUCUMBER SALAD *(p. 158)*
WITH BASIL AND HERB VINEGAR

BAKED BROWN BREAD *(p. 169)*

*For size servings on which data is based, see p. 12. To adjust fat level of menus, see p. 193.

Serves 6

Especially good with Kamut pasta (p. 20). Use part yogurt for sour cream if you're not freezing this dish.

1. Cook noodles *(p. 152 or 153)*:

    8 oz. whole grain noodles *(p. 20)*

2. In large fry pan over moderate heat, sauté nuts and vegetables in butter until vegetables are just crisp-tender:

    ¼ C. melted butter, unsalted   **½ C. celery, chopped**
    ¼ C. slivered or chopped almonds   **¼ C. onion, chopped**
    ¼ tsp. garlic powder

3. In small mixing bowl whisk together:

    1 C. light sour cream or sour cream *(p. 72)* **½ tsp. salt**
    ½ C. Parmesan cheese *(p. 72)*

4. Gently combine with sautéed ingredients:

    sour cream/cheese mixture   **1 tsp. lemon juice (blended into tuna)**
    cooked pasta   **½ C. frozen peas**
    6.5 oz. can tuna, water-packed, drained
       (50% reduced salt, *p. 30*)

VEGETARIAN ALTERNATIVE: Omit tuna. Increase to **1 C. frozen peas, 1 C. celery**; add **1 C. fresh sliced mushrooms** (sauté with vegetables in step 2) if desired.

19

SHOPPER'S GUIDE TO...
WHOLE GRAIN PASTAS

YOUR LOCAL HEALTH FOOD STORE IS THE PLACE TO LOOK FOR WONDERFUL PASTA VARIETIES!

WHOLE WHEAT

GOLDEN DURUM WHEAT: lighter whole wheat in texture.

SPELT: alternative for many wheat-allergic; similar to wheat in taste and texture; slightly nutty flavor; delicious!

KAMUT: alternative for wheat-allergic; lighter in texture; delicious, too! Our favorite! Seems like white flour pasta, yet higher in protein and minerals than whole wheat. Look for Kamut macaroni and noodles.

WHOLE WHEAT WITH VEGETABLE POWDERS OR OTHER GRAINS: wide range.

CORN SPAGHETTI (made from whole corn)

BROWN RICE SPAGHETTI

QUINOA: a highly nourishing gourmet grain.

MACARONI FROM UNBLEACHED WHITE FLOUR AND SOY OR SESAME: lighter than whole wheat; a good transition step if Kamut macaroni is not available.

SHOPPING LIST

• *Tamale Pie, p. 27* • *Best Burrito Beans, p. 25* • *Chicken Tetrazzini, p. 29*

MEATS/FISH/POULTRY:
ground turkey, 1 lb.
chicken, 1½ lbs. boneless breast

DAIRY:
butter, 2 sticks (or ¾ C. plus 1 tbsp.)
Parmesan cheese, 2 oz. (or ⅓ C.)
lowfat milk, ½ qt. (or 1¾ C.)

FRESH PRODUCE:
onions, 2 (1 small)
green pepper, 1 small

FROZEN:
corn, 10 oz. (2 C.)

STAPLES:
Check for ketchup, soy sauce, canola oil.

GRAINS/BEANS/PASTAS/NUTS:
*whole wheat pastry flour, ½ C.
*cornmeal, ½ lb. (1 C.)
*whole grain spaghetti, 10 oz.
 pinto or black beans, 1 lb. (2 C.)

CANNED FOODS/MISCELLANEOUS:
*chicken broth, 8 oz. (1 C.)
 tomato sauce, 16 oz. (2 C.)
  or *spaghetti or *pasta sauce
 mushroom stems/pieces, 4 oz. can
 sliced ripe olives, 2¼ oz. can
 diced green chilies, 4 oz. can, optional
 white grape juice, 2 oz. (¼ C.)
  or cooking sherry
 olive oil, 2 oz. (¼ C. in place of
 ½ stick butter), optional

SEASONINGS/HERBS:
Check *Herb and Spice Cupboard* (p. 5)
against recipes.

It may be necessary to purchase these items at a health food store.

21

Washing the Dishes

- *Fill the sink with hot soapy water as soon as you begin food preparation.*

- *Put in used items as you go.*

- *Stop periodically to wash, rinse, and drain the accumulation.*

- **BEST BURRITO BEANS,** *p. 25*
- **TAMALE PIE,** *p. 27*
- **CHICKEN TETRAZZINI,** *p. 29*

1. Crockpot cook beans night before.

2. Assemble ingredients for recipes on trays. Get out: large fry pan, large pan to cook pasta, pan to cook chicken, small saucepan for cornmeal topping, small mixing bowl to mix cornmeal and cold water, ovenproof baking dish for tamale pie, freezer containers.

3. For tetrazzini, start cooking chicken or have it cooked in advance with broth *(p. 145)*. Start heating water for noodles while chopping fresh ingredients.

4. Prepare fresh vegetables at the same time:
   - Chop 2 onions (1 small) for beans and tamale pie.
   - Chop green pepper for tamale pie.

5. Use the same fry pan to cook onions for beans, tamale pie filling, tetrazzini sauce, and assemble, in that order, washing out the pan as needed.

6. Complete each dish in order: beans, tamale pie ready to bake, tetrazzini (start browning ground turkey/vegetables for pie while completing beans).

7. Place in freezer containers, label, cool in refrigerator if needed, freeze. Include recipe page # on label to refer back to later.

BEST BURRITO BEANS

To thaw and reheat, see p. 8.

3/4 C. serving, *chilies included (approx. $.45)*
Exchanges: 0.75 meat, 0.75 fat, 3 bread, 0.75 vegetable
317 calories
18.5 grams protein (25%)
5 grams fat (15%), 12 mg. cholesterol (no cholesterol if olive oil is used)
47 grams carbohydrate (60%), 9.5 grams dietary fiber
432 mg. sodium

MENU

**599 Calories
28% Fat
$1.50***

BEST BURRITO BEANS (p. 25)

RADISHES, CUCUMBERS, CARROT STICKS

BURRITO FIXIN'S FOR 2 BURRITOS:

2 WHOLE WHEAT TORTILLAS (p. 164)

MOZZARELLA CHEESE (1/2 C.)

LETTUCE, TOMATOES, ONIONS

SALSA, YOGURT/SOUR CREAM

For size servings on which data is based, see p. 12. To adjust fat level of menus, see p. 193.

BEST BURRITO BEANS

4 Cups ~ Serves 5-6

Legumes are especially high in fiber and low in fat. Even with addition of butter or oil for extra flavor, the fat content of this recipe remains low.

1. Cook beans in crockpot overnight *(p. 147)* using:

   2 C. (1 lb.) raw pinto or black beans   **8 C. water**

2. Cook until onions are tender in unsalted butter or oil:

   ¹/₂ C. melted butter or olive oil *(p. 171)*   **2 tsp. cumin powder**
   1 onion, chopped   **¹/₄ tsp. garlic powder**
   1¹/₂ tbsp. chili powder

3. Drain cooked beans, reserving the liquid.

4. Mix onions into beans. Mash with potato ricer or electric mixer to desired consistency, adding reserved bean liquid as needed.

5. Mix in:

   4 oz. can diced green chilies, optional
   1 tsp. salt, to taste

6. **To Serve:** Top thawed, heated beans with **grated cheddar cheese**, or serve in **burritos** with **grated cheese, shredded lettuce, chopped tomatoes, salsa, whole wheat tortillas, light sour cream, etc.**

TAMALE PIE

To thaw and reheat, see p. 8.

1 serving of 6, with 90% fat-free ground turkey, tomato sauce and salt (approx. $.95)
    Exchanges: 2 meat, 0.75 fat, 1.75 bread, 1.5 vegetable
    300 calories
    20.5 grams protein (25%)
    9.5 grams fat (27%), 49 mg. cholesterol
    39 grams carbohydrate (48%), 8.5 grams dietary fiber
    508 mg. sodium

MENU

688 Calories
18% Fat
$1.80*

TAMALE PIE (p. 27)

FROZEN CORN

CARROT-RAISIN SALAD (p. 158)
WITH SWEET LITE DRESSING (p. 160)

YOGURT PIE (p. 188)

For size servings on which data is based, see p. 12. To adjust fat level of menus, see p. 193.

Serves 6

A winner with the whole family! Reheats best in a conventional oven.

Bake: 350° for 50-60 minutes, uncovered (9" baking pan or 2 qt. casserole dish)

1. Cook in large fry pan until turkey is browned and vegetables just tender:

1 lb. *Seasoned Ground Turkey* *(p. 149)*	**1 small green pepper, chopped**
1 small onion, chopped	**¹/₈ tsp. garlic powder**

2. Stir in, simmer briefly; pour into ovenproof baking pan or casserole:

2 C. tomato, spaghetti,	**2¹/₄ oz. can sliced ripe olives, drained**
or pasta sauce *(p. 94)*	**1¹/₂ tsp. chili powder**
¹/₂ tsp. salt (with tomato sauce only)	**2 C. frozen corn**

3. **Topping:** Whisk cornmeal into cold water; whisk into boiling water with butter and salt; cook and stir until thickened, about 2 minutes:

1 C. cold water	**1 tbsp. butter, unsalted**
1 C. stoneground cornmeal *(p. 177)*	**¹/₂ tsp. salt**
1 C. boiling water	

4. Spread hot cornmeal mixture evenly over top of pie mixture to the edges. Bake uncovered, *before* freezing, until crust is done. *To reheat*, cover, removing lid last 15-20 minutes to prevent a dried out or too soggy crust.

VEGETARIAN ALTERNATIVE: Omit ground turkey. Add **2 C. cooked lentils** or **15 oz. can drained kidney beans.** If desired, top with **1 C. grated cheddar cheese** just before cornmeal topping.

To thaw and reheat, see p. 8.

1 serving of 8 *(approx. $1.30)*
  Exchanges: 2.5 meat, 0.25 milk, 2.5 fat, 2.25 bread, 0.25 vegetable
  463 calories
  34 grams protein (30%)
  18.5 grams fat (36%), 88 mg. cholesterol
  36.5 grams carbohydrate (32%), 1.5 grams dietary fiber
  454 mg. sodium

MENU

804 Calories
29% Fat
$2.15*

CHICKEN TETRAZZINI *(p. 29)*

FROZEN OR FRESH GREEN BEANS

ARRANGED TOMATO/CUCUMBER SALAD *(p. 158)*
WITH BASIL AND HERB VINEGAR

BUTTERMILK DROP BISCUITS *(p. 180)*
WITH JAM

For size servings on which data is based, see p. 12. To adjust fat level of menus, see p. 193.

Serves 6-8

1. Cook spaghetti (p. 152 or 153):

   10 oz. whole grain spaghetti (p. 20)

2. **Sauce:** Blend flour into butter in large fry pan; cook and stir over medium heat about 1 minute; remove from heat; blend in milk and broth. Return to heat; cook and stir until thickened; blend in remaining ingredients:

   ¼ C. unsalted butter, melted
   ¼ C. canola oil or more butter
   ½ C. whole wheat pastry flour (p.163)
      (or 6 tbsp. unbleached white flour)
   1¾ C. lowfat milk
   ¼ C. white grape juice or cooking sherry

   1 C. chicken broth (p. 62 or 145)
   ½ tsp. salt
   ¼ tsp. pepper
   4 oz. can mushroom
      stems/pieces, drained

3. Fold together:

   sauce
   cooked spaghetti

   3 C. (1½ lbs.) cooked chicken (p. 145)
   ⅓ C. Parmesan cheese

VEGETARIAN ALTERNATIVE: Omit chicken and broth. Add **1 C. water** plus **1 tsp. *Sue's Kitchen Magic*** (p. 52), and **2 C. sliced fresh mushrooms**. Just before serving, fold in **½ C. minced fresh parsley**. Add **frozen peas**, if desired.

TUNA is available in white, light, chunk, flake, oil-pack, water-pack, no salt added, 50% salt-reduced, and regular. I recommend **WATER-PACK REGULAR CHUNK LIGHT TUNA** for balancing taste, cost, and nutrition. Unless on a salt-restricted diet, the sodium in an occasional can of tuna will not skyrocket your sodium intake. When using no-salt-added or 50% salt-reduced tuna, the addition of lemon juice will improve the flavor.

CANNED SALMON is a good alternative to fresh salmon, although it's high in sodium. Pink salmon is generally more economical than red salmon, but you'll want to choose pink or red according to your taste preference. Salmon contains high quality heart-protective omega-3 fatty acids. Unless on a salt-restricted diet, occasional use of canned salmon will not send your sodium intake beyond acceptable limits.

FREEZER SET #3

• *Tuna or Salmon Loaf, p. 35* • *Emilie's Noodle Bake, p. 37* • *Chicken Hawaiian, p. 39*

MEATS/FISH/POULTRY:
ground turkey, 1 lb.
chicken, 1 lb. boneless breast
tuna, water-pack, 2—6.5 oz. cans
   or salmon, 15.5 oz. can

DAIRY:
lowfat milk, 1/2 C.
eggs, 3 large
lowfat cottage cheese, 1 pt.

FRESH PRODUCE:
celery, 3 C.
2 onions, 1 medium plus 1/4 C.

FROZEN:
frozen peas, 3 oz. (1/2 C.)

GRAINS/BEANS/PASTAS/NUTS:
*spinach noodles, 8 oz.
*cashews, roasted, unsalted, 1/2 C.

CANNED FOODS/MISCELLANEOUS:
*pasta or spaghetti sauce, 2 C.
Shredded Wheat, small box
pimiento, 2 oz. jar
pineapple chunks, 20 oz. can

STAPLES:
Check for olive oil, lemon juice, ketchup,
soy sauce, apple cider vinegar, honey,
lemon juice, cornstarch or arrowroot
powder.

SEASONINGS/HERBS:
Check *Herb and Spice Cupboard, (p. 5)*
against recipes.

*It may be necessary to purchase these items at a health food store.

Creating Cracker Crumbs

*S*o you have a recipe that calls for crushed saltine or soda crackers? *Shredded Wheat* (whole wheat and no salt) makes a perfect alternative!

•

Four large *Shredded Wheat* biscuits ground in the blender makes about 1 C. "cracker" crumbs.

•

In a pinch you can use whole wheat bread crumbs ground from dry bread in the blender.

- **TUNA OR SALMON LOAF,** *p. 35*
- **EMILIE'S NOODLE BAKE,** *p. 37*
- **CHICKEN HAWAIIAN,** *p. 39*

1. Assemble ingredients for recipes on separate trays. Get out: 1 large fry pan, large pan to cook noodles, pan to cook chicken, 1 small and 1 large mixing bowl, medium loaf pan, blender, electric mixer, freezer containers.

2. Use the same fry pan for *Noodle Bake* and *Chicken Hawaiian*, washing pan out as needed.

3. For *Chicken Hawaiian*, start cooking chicken or have it cooked in advance *(p. 145)*. Start heating water for noodles. Season ground turkey and start browning it while preparing fresh vegetables.

4. Prepare fresh vegetables and crumbs at the same time:
    - Slice 1 medium onion, chop ¼ C. onion.
    - Diagonally slice 2 C. celery, finely chop 1 C. celery.
    - 1 C. *Shredded Wheat* or dry bread crumbs in blender *(p. 32)*.

5. Complete each dish in order: *Tuna or Salmon Loaf* to bake, *Noodle Bake*, *Chicken Hawaiian*.

6. Place in freezer containers, label, cool in refrigerator if needed, freeze. Include recipe page # on label to refer back to later.

✿ TUNA OR SALMON LOAF ✿

To thaw and reheat, see p. 8.

1 serving of 6, *Tuna Loaf (approx. $.55)*
Exchanges: 2 meat, 0.5 bread, 0.5 vegetable
160 calories
20.5 grams protein (49%)
4.5 grams fat (23%), 143 mg. cholesterol
11.5 grams carbohydrate (28%), 2 grams dietary fiber
580 mg. sodium

MENU

553 Calories
35% Fat
$1.45*

TUNA OR SALMON LOAF *(p. 35)*
WITH LEMON WEDGE

6 OZ. BAKED POTATO *(p. 137)*
**WITH 2 TBSP. LOWFAT SOUR CREAM
AND 1 TBSP. BUTTER SPREAD** *(p. 171)*

STEAMED SPINACH

ORANGE-LETTUCE-BANANA SALAD *(p. 158)*
WITH SWEET LITE DRESSING *(p. 160)*

For size servings on which data is based, see p. 12. To adjust fat level of menus, see p. 193.

TUNA OR SALMON LOAF

My favorite economy fish dish. I make 2 loaves, cutting them in half for 4 freezer meals.

Bake: 350° for 1 hour, uncovered (8¹/₂" x 4¹/₂" loaf pan)

1. In large mixing bowl, thoroughly mix together:

¹/₂ C. *Shredded Wheat,* **fine crumbs** *(p. 32),* **or dried whole grain bread crumbs**	¹/₄ C. chopped onion
	2 tsp. lemon juice
¹/₂ C. lowfat milk	2 oz. jar pimiento,
1 C. celery, chopped fine	drained, chopped
2—6.5 oz. cans tuna, water-packed, or 15.5 oz. can salmon *(p. 30)*	¹/₂ tsp. salt

   (drain well, thoroughly break up with fingers)

2. Separate eggs. Blend yolks into tuna mixture. Beat whites until stiff (but not dry) and fold thoroughly, but gently, into tuna mixture:

   3 large egg yolks   **3 large egg whites, whipped**

3. Pile tuna mixture evenly into loaf pan sprayed with nonstick spray. Bake uncovered until firm. Cool in refrigerator thoroughly before freezing.

4. **To Freeze and Reheat:** See *Meat Loaf,* p. 99, steps 4 and 5.

VARIATION: To serve freshly baked, without freezing, place **6 thin half-slices fresh lemon** in bottom of loaf pan before adding tuna mixture. Loosen sides of loaf and invert on platter. Garnish with **parsley sprigs** and serve with extra lemon.

♦ EMILIE'S NOODLE BAKE ♦

To thaw and reheat, see p. 8.

1 serving of 6, *using 90% fat-free ground turkey (approx. $1.10)*
Exchanges: 3 meat, 0.25 fat, 1.75 bread, 2 vegetable
364 calories
32.5 grams protein (36%)
9.5 grams fat (24%), 50 mg. cholesterol
37 grams carbohydrate (40%), 8 grams dietary fiber
738 mg. sodium

M E N U

704 Calories
28% Fat
$1.90*

EMILIE'S NOODLE BAKE (p. 37)

TOSSED SALAD (p. 158)
WITH SWEET LITE DRESSING (p. 160)

SOURDOUGH BREAD (p. 162)
WITH BUTTER SPREAD (p. 171)

APPLE WEDGES

For size servings on which data is based, see p. 12. To adjust fat level of menus, see p. 193.

A really simple casserole with 4 ingredients!

1. Cook pasta *(p. 152 or 153)*:

   8 oz. package spinach noodles *(p. 20)*

2. In large fry pan brown turkey and combine with remaining ingredients:

   1 lb. *Seasoned Ground Turkey* *(p. 149)*
   2 C. pasta or spaghetti sauce *(p. 94)*
   1 pt. lowfat cottage cheese
   cooked spinach noodles

VEGETARIAN ALTERNATIVE: Omit ground turkey; sauté in a small amount of **olive oil** and add to sauce: **1 small chopped green pepper, 1 diced carrot, 1 small chopped onion, ½ C. diced celery.** If desired add just before serving and heat to melt: **1 C. grated cheddar cheese.**

❧ CHICKEN HAWAIIAN ❧

To thaw and reheat, see p. 8.

1 serving of 6 *(approx. $1.40)*
>   *Exchanges: 2 meat, 2 fat, 1 bread, 1.5 fruit, 1 vegetable*
>   *349 calories*
>   *30 grams protein (29%)*
>   *10 grams fat (25%), 58 mg. cholesterol*
>   *40.5 grams carbohydrate (46%), 4.5 grams dietary fiber*
>   *304 mg. sodium*

MENU

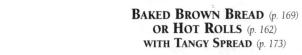

CHICKEN HAWAIIAN *(p. 39)*

BROWN RICE *(p. 148)*

CARROT-RAISIN SALAD *(p. 158)*
WITH SWEET MAYONNAISE DRESSING *(p. 160)*

BAKED BROWN BREAD *(p. 169)*
OR HOT ROLLS *(p. 162)*
WITH TANGY SPREAD *(p. 173)*

---

*For size servings on which data is based, see p. 12. To adjust fat level of menus, see p. 193.

Serve over chow mein noodles and/or brown rice.

1. In large fry pan sauté vegetables in oil until crisp-tender, about 4 minutes:

   1 tbsp. olive oil *(p. 171)* **1 medium onion, sliced,**
   2 C. celery, sliced thinly on diagonal **separated into rings**

2. **Sauce:** Whisk together in small mixing bowl, stir into vegetables and cook while stirring, until thickened over medium heat, about 1 minute:

   1 C. pineapple juice plus water **$\frac{1}{3}$ C. apple cider vinegar**
   (juice drained from chunks, **$\frac{1}{4}$ C. honey**
   step 3 below) *(p. 94)* **$\frac{1}{2}$ tsp. powdered ginger**
   2 tbsp. soy sauce *(p. 94)* **2 tbsp. cornstarch***

3. Remove from heat and fold in:

   2 C. (1 lb.) cooked chicken, small chunks *(p. 145)*
   2 oz. jar pimiento, drained, chopped
   20 oz. can pineapple chunks, unsweetened, drained
   $\frac{1}{2}$ C. cashews, roasted, unsalted *(p. 146)*
   $\frac{1}{2}$ C. frozen green peas

*Arrowroot powder may be substituted (purchase at health food store).

VEGETARIAN ALTERNATIVE: Omit chicken. Add **1 C. cashews**, **1 C. peas**, and **10 oz. firm tofu,** drained, cut in 1" cubes *(p. 82)*.

SHOPPER'S GUIDE TO...
RICE

AVAILABLE IN SUPERMARKETS

LONG GRAIN BROWN RICE—texture most pleasing for white rice lovers.

MEDIUM GRAIN—texture more moist and chewy.

UNCLE BEN'S CONVERTED WHITE RICE—virtually nil in fiber, but higher in nutrients than regular white rice because some nutrients are added in processing. A better alternative to white rice if you dislike the brown.

AVAILABLE IN HEALTH FOOD STORES

LONG GRAIN, SHORT GRAIN—inorganic or organic.*

BASMATI RICE*—white and brown with a special flavor!

VARIETY PACKS—e.g., red with wild, with brown, etc.

*For mail order source, see p. 146.

FREEZER SET #4

Black Beans, p. 45 • Mexican Rice, p. 47 • Chicken Pot Pie, p. 49
• Sweet 'n Sour Meatballs, p. 51

MEATS/FISH/POULTRY:
ground turkey, 1 lb.
chicken, 1½ lbs. boneless breast

DAIRY:
nonfat milk, 1½ C.
eggs, 2 large
butter, ¼ C. (½ stick)

FRESH PRODUCE:
onions, 3 medium
green pepper, 1
    (plus 1 optional, see step 5, p. 51)
garlic, 2 cloves, optional
carrots, ½ lb. (or 3 medium)
celery, 4 ribs

FROZEN:
frozen peas, 10 oz. (2 C.)

GRAINS/BEANS/PASTAS/NUTS:
*whole wheat pastry flour, ¼ lb.
*cornmeal, ¼ lb. (¾ C.)
brown rice, ½ lb. (1 C.)
    or *Uncle Ben's Converted Rice*
black beans, 1 lb. (2¼ C.)
wheat germ, toasted, ¼ C.

CANNED FOODS/MISCELLANEOUS:
*chicken broth, 27 oz. (3⅜ C.)
wine vinegar, ¼ C.
tomato juice, 6 oz. can
pineapple juice, 6 oz. can
pineapple chunks, 20 oz. can

STAPLES:
Check for olive oil, honey, ketchup,
soy sauce, apple cider vinegar, cornstarch,
crystalline fructose or sugar, baking powder.

SEASONINGS/HERBS:
Check *Herb and Spice Cupboard* (p. 5)
against recipes.

It may be necessary to purchase these items at a health food store.

41

A variety of fat levels of ground turkey are available, depending on how much skin is added and the proportion of light and dark meat used. Percentages such as 85%, 90%, 93%, and 99% "fat-free" are by weight, not by calories. For example, 90% fat-free ground turkey is 10% fat by weight, but 45% fat by calories. So don't be fooled!

Even so, ground turkey is still a good alternative to ground beef. It is lower in calories, fat, and cholesterol (including lean ground beef), and is easier to digest. Choose the lowest fat level you can find that is appealing in texture and flavor. The seasoning for ground turkey on p. 149 helps! I use 99% fat-free when I can find it. However, since 90% fat-free is more widely available, I have used this level in the nutrient data of *Meals in Minutes* recipes.

- **BLACK BEANS,** *p. 45*
- **MEXICAN RICE,** *p. 47*
- **CHICKEN POT PIE,** *p. 49*
- **SWEET 'N SOUR MEATBALLS,** *p. 51*

1. Assemble ingredients for recipes on trays. Get out: 1 large fry pan, 2 medium saucepans (1 with lid) to cook rice and chicken, 1 small saucepan, 1 small and 1 large mixing bowl, freezer containers, ovenproof casserole for chicken pot pie.

2. For pot pie, start cooking chicken or have it cooked in advance with broth (p. 145).

3. Prepare fresh vegetables at the same time:
    - Chop 3 medium onions—1 each for beans and pie; 1 for rice and meatballs (¹/₄ C. of it).
    - Dice 1 green pepper.
    - Chop 4 ribs celery.
    - Slice or coarsely chop 2 carrots; finely chop 1 carrot.
    - Mince 2 cloves garlic, optional (step 2, p. 45).

4. Use the same fry pan to cook in order: vegetables for beans, sauté rice, pie filling, meatballs, washing pan out as needed.

5. Complete each dish in order: beans, rice to cook, pie to bake, meatballs. Cook the rice, bake the chicken pot pie.

6. Place in freezer containers, label, cool in refrigerator if needed, freeze. Include recipe page # on label to refer back to later.

BLACK BEANS

To thaw and reheat, see p. 8.

1 C. serving *(approx. $.45)*
  Exchanges: 1.25 meat, 3.25 bread, 2.75 fat
  500 calories
  23 grams protein (18%)
  14 grams fat (24%), 0 mg. cholesterol
  86 grams carbohydrate (58%), 12.5 grams dietary fiber
  738 mg. sodium (with 1½ tsp. salt in recipe)

MENU

927 Calories
31% Fat
$.95*

1 C. BLACK BEANS *(p. 45)*

2 PIECES CORNBREAD *(p. 178)*
WITH HONEY BUTTER SPREAD *(p. 173)*

WALDORF SALAD *(p. 158)*
OR
SCRAMBLED EGGS

ARRANGED TOMATO /CUCUMBER
OR AVOCADO SLICE SALAD *(p. 158)*
WITH BASIL AND HERB VINEGAR

*For size servings on which data is based, see p. 12. To adjust fat level of menus, see p. 193.

BLACK BEANS

We love these beans! With whole grains, beans provide an economical complete protein.

1. Cook beans in crockpot overnight *(p. 147)* using:

   2¼ C. black (turtle) beans (1 lb.)

2. In large fry pan sauté onions and garlic in oil:

   ¼ C. olive oil *(p. 171)*   **2 cloves garlic, minced**
   1 medium onion, chopped   **or ¼ tsp. garlic powder**
   1 green pepper, diced

3. Drain liquid from cooked beans, leaving a small portion as desired in beans; add and continue cooking 20 minutes:

   sautéed onion and garlic   **2 tbsp. honey**
   ¼ C. wine vinegar   **½ tsp. cumin powder**

4. Season with:

   up to 1½ tsp. salt, to taste

5. **Optional:** Blend some or all of the beans in electric mixer for desired refried bean consistency.

VARIATION: Omit green pepper in step 2. **To Serve:** Lightly steam or sauté **chopped green pepper** and add just before serving. This will preserve its bright green color!

45

To thaw and reheat, see p. 8.

½ C. serving *(approx. $.20)*
Exchanges: 0.25 fat, 1 bread, 0.5 vegetable
101 calories
2 grams protein (8%)
2 grams fat (17%), 0 mg. cholesterol
19.5 grams carbohydrate (75%), 0.5 gram dietary fiber
216 mg. sodium

MENU

718 Calories
23% Fat
$.95*

MEXICAN RICE *(p. 47)*
¾ C. BLACK BEANS *(p. 45)*
1 WHOLE WHEAT TORTILLA *(p. 162)*
SHREDDED LETTUCE
SALSA
¼ C. YOGURT/SOUR CREAM
(HALF OF EACH)
PINEAPPLE WEDGES

*For size servings on which data is based, see p. 12. To adjust fat level of menus, see p. 193.

Delicious, especially with black beans. Brown rice may be substituted for converted white rice. I enjoy serving whole wheat tortillas with this dish and the black beans.

1. In large fry pan sauté rice, onion, and carrot in oil over moderately high heat, stirring often to brown rice evenly and prevent burning:

   1 tbsp. canola or olive oil *(p. 171)*   **½ small onion, chopped**
   1 C. *Uncle Ben's Converted White*   **1 medium carrot, finely diced**
      Rice or long grain brown rice

2. In medium saucepan that has a tight-fitting lid, bring to a boil:

   about 14.5 oz. can (or 1⅞ C.) chicken broth *(p. 62)*
   6 oz. can tomato juice
   1½ tsp. cumin powder

3. Stir rice mixture into boiling liquid. Immediately cover converted rice, or moderately boil brown rice uncovered for 5 minutes and cover tightly. Reduce heat very low and simmer—converted rice for 25 minutes or brown rice for 60-65 minutes, or until all the liquid is absorbed. Fold in:

   ½ tsp. dried cilantro or finely chopped fresh cilantro, to taste

VEGETARIAN ALTERNATIVES: Omit broth. Add **2 C. water** plus **2 tsp. of *Sue's Kitchen Magic*** *(p. 52)*.

To thaw and reheat, see p. 8.

1 serving of 6, with low sodium baking powder, butter for sautéeing excluded (approx. $1.50)
 Exchanges: 3 meat, 0.25 milk, 1 fat, 2.5 bread, 1 vegetable
 465 calories
 43.5 grams protein (37%)
 12 grams fat (23%), 139 mg. cholesterol
 47.5 grams carbohydrate (40%), 10.5 grams dietary fiber
 808 mg. sodium

MENU

721 Calories
16% Fat
$1.90*

CHICKEN POT PIE (p. 49)

BROWN RICE (p. 148)

ORANGE-LETTUCE-BANANA SALAD (p. 158)
WITH SWEET LITE DRESSING (p. 160)

For size servings on which data is based, see p. 12. To adjust fat level of menus, see p. 193.

Bake: 350° for 30-40 minutes, uncovered (2-2½ qt. ovenproof casserole)

1. **Filling:** In large fry pan sauté vegetables in unsalted butter or water about 7 minutes; add remaining ingredients, bring to boil; remove from heat:

½ stick (¼ C.) butter, melted, optional	**1½ C. chicken broth** *(p. 62 or 145)*
1 medium onion, chopped	**¾ tsp. salt**
4 ribs celery, chopped	**¼ tsp. pepper**
2 carrots, sliced or coarsely chopped	**¼ tsp. thyme**

2. In small mixing bowl whisk flour into milk; blend into broth mixture, stirring until thickened; add peas and chicken:

1 C. nonfat milk	**3 C. (1½ lbs.) chicken** *(p. 145)*
¼ C. whole wheat pastry flour *(p. 163)*	**10 oz. (2 C.) frozen peas**

3. **Crust:** In medium mixing bowl blend dry ingredients, cut in butter until crumbly; combine and stir in liquids until moistened:

¾ C. stoneground cornmeal *(p. 177)*	**¾ tsp. salt**
¾ C. whole wheat pastry flour	**3 tbsp. soft butter**
1½ tsp. crystalline fructose *(p. 163)*	**1 large egg, beaten**
1½ tsp. baking powder *(p. 163)*	**½ C. nonfat milk**

4. In casserole, spread crust evenly over filling. Bake until crust is done.

VEGETARIAN ALTERNATIVE: Omit broth and chicken. Add **1½ C. water** plus **1½ tsp. *Sue's Kitchen Magic*** *(p. 52)*, **2 C. fresh mushroom pieces, 5 ribs chopped celery, 3 medium carrots.**

SWEET 'N SOUR MEATBALLS

To thaw and reheat, see p. 8.

6 meatballs with sauce, pineapple, green pepper, using 90% fat-free ground turkey (approx. $1.35)

> Exchanges: 3 meat, 2 bread, 3 fruit, 0.75 vegetable
> 454 calories
> 29 grams protein (24%)
> 10.5 grams fat (20%), 119 mg. cholesterol
> 66 grams carbohydrate (56%), 3.5 grams dietary fiber
> 494 mg. sodium

MENU

895 Calories
20% Fat
$1.40*

SWEET 'N SOUR MEATBALLS (p. 51)
OVER
WHOLE GRAIN NOODLES (p. 152)

FANTASTIC BROCCOLI (p. 156)

CARROT-RAISIN SALAD (p. 158)
WITH **SWEET MAYONNAISE DRESSING** (p. 160)

For size servings on which data is based, see p. 12. To adjust fat level of menus, see p. 193.

SWEET 'N SOUR MEATBALLS

A savory meat! Serve over brown rice or whole grain cooked noodles.

1. In mixing bowl combine in order given and shape into 24 balls:

1 beaten egg	**¹/₂ tsp. salt, optional**
¹/₄ C. onion, finely chopped	**¹/₂ tsp. pepper**
¹/₄ C. toasted wheat germ	**1 lb. *Seasoned Ground Turkey*** (p. 149)

2. In moderately hot large fry pan brown meatballs, turning gently. Add, bring to boil, cover, reduce heat, and simmer 15 minutes:

   ¹/₃ C. pineapple juice, unsweetened (from 6 oz. can juice)

3. **Sauce:** In small saucepan whisk together, bring to boil while stirring constantly with whisk until thickened, about 1 minute:

remaining juice from 6 oz. can	**2¹/₂ tbsp. cornstarch**
juice drained from 20 oz. can	**1¹/₂ tbsp. soy sauce** (p. 94)
pineapple chunks	**¹/₄ C. plus 1 tbsp. honey**
³/₈ C. plus 2 tsp. vinegar	**⁵/₈ tsp. ginger**

4. Combine meatballs, sauce, and:

   pineapple chunks (from 20 oz. can)

5. **To Serve:** If desired, lightly sauté and add **1 green pepper**, cut in strips.

VEGETARIAN ALTERNATIVE: Prepare just the **sauce**. It is yummy stirred into **stir-fry vegetables**, or served over rice plain or with **cashews and/or tofu cubes** added.

Sue's Kitchen Magic Seasoning is a special soy protein blend with alfalfa, corn, and wheat. It contains no MSG. It imparts a fantastic flavor to many recipes as an alternative to chicken broth. In fact, it tastes better! It is not sodium-free, but it does reduce the need for salt and is lower in sodium than chicken broth or bouillon. One teaspoon contains 710 mg. sodium compared to 2,132 mg. in a teaspoon of salt. It is an all-vegetable product.

This seasoning is available by mail order from *Eating Better Cookbooks* (address on p. 210).

SHOPPING LIST

FREEZER SET #5
• *Lentil Rice Casserole, p. 57* • *Turkey-Mushroom Sauce, p. 59* • *Chicken Spaghetti, p. 61*

MEATS/FISH/POULTRY:
ground turkey, 1 lb.
chicken, 1½ lbs. boneless breast

DAIRY:
sour cream or lowfat yogurt, 1 C.,
    optional, see step 4, p. 59

FRESH PRODUCE:
onions, 2 small (plus 1 optional for lentil
    rice)
green pepper, 1, optional, see step 2, p. 61
mushrooms, ⅓ lb. (2 C.), optional
    or canned (see *Canned Foods*)

STAPLES:
Check for *Sue's Kitchen Magic*, olive oil, dry
or fresh parsley (optional), ketchup, soy
sauce.

GRAINS/BEANS/PASTAS/NUTS:
*whole grain spaghetti, 8 oz.
*whole wheat pastry flour, ¾ C.
 lentils, ½ lb. (or ¾ C.)
 brown rice, ¼ lb. (½ C.)

CANNED FOODS/MISCELLANEOUS:
*chicken broth, 16 oz. (2 C.)
        plus 24 oz. (3 C.), optional,
        step 1, p. 57
small jar instant minced onion flakes, or
        fresh onion (see *Fresh Produce*)
mushrooms, 2—4 oz. cans, optional
        or fresh (see *Fresh Produce*)
tomato sauce, 15 oz. can
stewed tomatoes, 1 lb. can

SEASONINGS/HERBS:
Check *Herb and Spice Cupboard* (p. 5)
against recipes.

*It may be necessary to purchase these items at a health food store.

Parsley Pickin's

Store the bunch upright with stems in a jar of water;
cover loosely with plastic bag. Keeps this way in refrigerator
up to 3 weeks! Change water a time or two.

•

Mince easily with chef's knife or in blender.
Use on lots of dishes and salads!

•

Parsley doesn't keep its color when frozen,
so add to freezer dishes just before serving.

•

Fantastically high in vitamins A and C plus breath-freshening
chlorophyll. Try munching it. It can really taste good!

ASSEMBLY TIPS

LENTIL RICE CASSEROLE, *p. 57*
TURKEY-MUSHROOM SAUCE, *p. 59*
CHICKEN SPAGHETTI, *p. 61*

1. Assemble ingredients for recipes on trays. Get out: 1 large fry pan, large pan to cook pasta, pan to cook chicken and *Turkey-Mushroom Sauce*, ovenproof casserole for lentil rice, freezer containers.

2. For *Chicken Spaghetti*, start cooking chicken or have it cooked in advance with broth (p. 145).

3. Start heating water for spaghetti. Season and start browning ground turkey for *Turkey-Mushroom Sauce*.

4. Prepare fresh vegetables at the same time:
   • Chop 2 small onions (plus 1 optional for lentil rice, step 1, p. 57).
   • Chop 1 green pepper, optional (step 2, p. 61).
   • Slice 1 or 2 C. fresh mushrooms, optional (step 1, p. 59; step 2, p. 61).

5. Use the same fry pan to cook *Turkey-Mushroom* and *Chicken Spaghetti* sauce, washing pan out as needed.

6. Complete each dish in order: *Lentil Rice* for baking, *Turkey-Mushroom Sauce*, *Chicken Spaghetti*.

7. Place in freezer containers, label, cool in refrigerator if needed, freeze. Include recipe page # on label to refer back to later.

❧ LENTIL RICE CASSEROLE ❧

To thaw and reheat, see p. 8.

³/₄ C. serving, *cheese not included (approx. $.35)*
Exchanges: 0.75 meat, 3 bread
242 calories
12 grams protein (19%)
1 gram fat (4%), 0 mg. cholesterol
47 grams carbohydrate, 6.5 grams dietary fiber
548 mg. sodium

MENU

LENTIL RICE CASSEROLE *(p. 57)*
WITH 3 TBSP. GRATED CHEDDAR CHEESE
BURRITO STYLE

OR WITH *TOSSED SALAD *(p. 158)*
WITH LEMON-OLIVE OIL DRESSING *(p. 161)*

STEAMED PARSLEYED CARROTS
WITH 1 TSP. BUTTER

ORANGE AMBROSIA *(p. 182)*

Data for second menu selection. For size servings on which data is based, see p. 12. To adjust fat level of menus, see p. 193.

♨♨ LENTIL RICE CASSEROLE ♨♨

Takes 5 minutes to assemble! A great recipe—especially tasty in burritos. You may be wondering if this dish can be cooked in a crockpot. Not if you want a pleasing texture.

Bake: 300° for 2-2½ hours, covered (1 qt. ovenproof casserole)

1. Combine in casserole dish:

¾ C. dry lentils
½ C. uncooked brown rice
(long grain gives best texture)
¼ C. instant minced onion flakes
or 1 small onion, chopped
1 tbsp. *Sue's Kitchen Magic* *(p. 52)*

½ tsp. sweet basil leaves
¼ tsp. oregano leaves
¼ tsp. thyme leaves
¼ tsp. garlic powder
3 C. water*

2. Cover; bake until rice and lentils are tender. Casserole may easily be removed from baking dish to freezer container or containers.

3. **To Serve** (optional): Just before serving, top hot casserole with cheese and stir in to melt (for burritos) or serve unmelted cheese separately:

¾ C. grated cheddar cheese (may be grated and frozen in a separate package, if desired)

4. Garnish with **finely chopped fresh parsley.**

3 C. chicken broth may be used in place of **Kitchen Magic and **water**, but dish will not be as tasty.*

TURKEY-MUSHROOM SAUCE

To thaw and reheat, see p. 8.

¾ C. serving, *with half sour cream, half lowfat yogurt, 90% fat-free ground turkey (approx. $.80)*
  Exchanges: 1.75 meat, 1 fat, 1 milk, 1 bread, 0.5 vegetable
  233 calories
  19 grams protein (31%)
  9 grams fat (35%), 48 mg. cholesterol
  21 grams carbohydrate (34%), 2 grams dietary fiber
  879 mg. sodium

MENU

528 Calories
18% Fat
$1.95*

TURKEY-MUSHROOM SAUCE (p. 59)

8 OZ. BAKED POTATO (p. 137)

FROZEN OR FRESH GREEN PEAS

ARRANGED TOMATO/CUCUMBER SALAD (p. 158)
WITH BASIL AND HERB VINEGAR

*For size servings on which data is based, see p. 12. To adjust fat level of menus, see p. 193.

TURKEY-MUSHROOM SAUCE

5 Cups ~ Serves 6-8

*Serve over baked potatoes, whole grain toast, brown rice, or **Buttermilk Drop Biscuits** (p. 180).*

1. Mix together and brown in large fry pan:

   1 lb. *Seasoned Ground Turkey* (p. 149)   **4 oz. can mushrooms**
   1 small onion, chopped   **or 1 C. fresh sliced mushrooms**

2. **Sauce:** In medium saucepan whisk together until smooth, bring to boil while stirring constantly, and cook until thickened:

   2 C. cold chicken broth (p. 62 or 145)   **1 tsp. garlic powder**
   ³/₄ C. whole wheat pastry flour (p. 163)   **2 tbsp. *Sue's Kitchen Magic*** (p. 52), **optional**
   (or 6 tbsp. unbleached flour)

3. Fold sauce into cooked turkey mixture.

4. **To Serve** (optional): Blend into thawed sauce before reheating (do not allow to boil):

   1 C. light sour cream or lowfat yogurt (or ¹/₂ C. each blended)
   2 tsp. dry or ¹/₄ C. fresh minced parsley

VEGETARIAN ALTERNATIVE: Omit ground turkey and broth. Add: **2 C. fresh sliced mushrooms, 1 C. frozen peas, 2 C. cold water plus 2 tbsp. *Sue's Kitchen Magic*.**

59

CHICKEN SPAGHETTI

To thaw and reheat, see p. 8.

1 serving of 6 *(approx. $1.70)*
   Exchanges: 2.75 meat, 1 fat, 2 bread, 2.5 vegetable
   413 calories
   40 grams protein (40%)
   8.5 grams fat (19%), 87 mg. cholesterol
   42 grams carbohydrate (41%), 3.5 grams dietary fiber
   540 mg. sodium

MENU

742 Calories
23% Fat
$2.60*

CHICKEN SPAGHETTI *(p. 61)*
WITH 1 TBSP. PARMESAN CHEESE

STEAMED ZUCCHINI

ARRANGED ORANGE/PINEAPPLE SALAD *(p. 158)*
WITH SWEET LITE DRESSING *(p. 160)*

SOURDOUGH BREAD *(p. 164)*
WITH 1 TBSP. BUTTER SPREAD *(p. 171)*

*For size servings on which data is based, see p. 12. To adjust fat level of menus, see p. 193.

About 2-2½ Quart Casserole ~ Serves 6-8

A lowfat dish refreshingly different from spaghetti with hamburger.

1. Cook spaghetti *(p. 152 or 153)*:

   8 oz. whole grain spaghetti *(p. 20)*

2. In large fry pan sauté vegetables in oil or butter until barely tender:

   2 tbsp. olive oil *(p. 171)*   **1 green pepper, chopped, optional**
   1 small onion, chopped   **4 oz. can mushrooms**
                                            or 1 C. fresh sliced mushrooms

3. Stir in and cook over low heat for 5 minutes:

   15 oz. can tomato sauce   **1 tsp. Italian seasoning**
   1 lb. can stewed tomatoes   **½ tsp. salt**

4. Add chicken, stirring carefully so chicken does not break up; cook 5-10 minutes:

   3 C. cooked chicken, coarsely shredded pieces *(p. 145)*

5. Layer sauce with chicken on top of spaghetti in casserole dish to freeze.

VARIATION: Use 1-1½ lbs. *Seasoned Ground Turkey (p. 149)* in place of chicken.

VEGETARIAN ALTERNATIVE: Omit chicken. Add **2-3 C. cooked lentils** or **kidney beans.**

SHOPPER'S GUIDE TO...
CHICKEN AND CHICKEN BROTH

CHICKEN: The best brands of chicken are grown without hormones and chemicals. Request this information where you buy poultry in your area. For convenience and lowest fat content, boneless breast is best. The costs of *Meals in Minutes* recipes are based on using it. A considerable savings can be realized, however, by using whole chicken in place of boneless breast. For example, boneless breast at $3.79 per lb. yields about 1⅝ cups cooked, skinned chicken ($2.35 per cup). A 3½ lb. whole chicken at $.99 per lb. yields about 3¼ cups cooked, skinned chicken ($1.07 per cup).

CHICKEN BROTH: Bouillon cubes are very high in sodium and contain MSG (monosodium glutamate). Some brands of canned broth are reduced in sodium or omit MSG. *Pritikin* brand is sometimes available in super-markets. *Hain* and *Health Valley* brands are available in health food stores and sometimes in supermarkets. These brands offer unsalted and salted broth, without MSG. As far as a vegetarian "chicken-like" flavor substitute for chicken broth, we haven't found any we like. *Sue's Kitchen Magic* *(p. 52)* best serves this purpose in terms of flavor. Price-wise, it's most economical to make your own delicious broth while cooking whole chickens or less expensive parts *(p. 145)*.

FREEZER SET #6
Creole Peas 'n Corn, p. 67 • Chicken Rice Pilaf, p. 69 • Noodles Parmesan, p. 71

MEATS/FISH/POULTRY:
chicken, 1 lb. boneless breast

DAIRY:
butter, 1½ sticks, optional,
  see steps 3 and 4, p. 67; step 1, p. 69;
    step 2, p. 71
sour cream, ½ pt. (1 C.)
Parmesan cheese, 3 oz. (½ C.)

FRESH PRODUCE:
onion, 1
green pepper, 1
mushrooms, ¼ lb. (or 1 C.), optional
  or canned (see *Canned Foods*)
zucchini, 1 small
broccoli for 1 C. flowers
garlic, 2 cloves

GRAINS/BEANS/PASTAS/NUTS:
*whole grain noodles, 8 oz.

black-eyed peas, 1 lb. (2 C.)
brown rice, 1 lb. (or 1½ C.)
almonds, 2 oz. (¼ C.)
  slivered or whole

CANNED FOODS/MISCELLANEOUS:
stewed tomatoes, 1 lb. can
tomato sauce, 8 oz. can
sliced water chestnuts, 8 oz. can
mushrooms, 4 oz. can, optional
  or fresh (see *Fresh Produce*)

FROZEN:
frozen corn, 10 oz. (or 1½ C.)

STAPLES:
Check for honey, *Sue's Kitchen Magic*,
Worcestershire or soy sauce.

SEASONINGS/HERBS:
Check *Herb and Spice Cupboard* (p. 5)
against recipes.

*It may be necessary to purchase these items at a health food store.

63

A Bit O'Butter

A little butter adds a touch of yummy flavor
without sending the fat level "out of sight."

•

The saturated fat of butter is better for you than the
hydrogenated fat of margarine—in small amounts.

•

Use lightly salted butter for spreads. For baking and cooking,
use unsalted butter to reduce sodium. See p. 6 for storage tips.

CREOLE PEAS 'N CORN, *p. 67*
CHICKEN RICE PILAF, *p. 69*
NOODLES PARMESAN, *p. 71*

1. Soak black-eyed peas for creole in large pan in advance or overnight.

2. Assemble ingredients for recipes on trays. Get out: 1 large fry pan, large pan to cook pasta and black-eyed peas, medium saucepan to cook chicken and rice, small mixing bowl, freezer containers.

3. For pilaf, start cooking chicken or have it cooked in advance *(p. 145)*. Start heating water for noodles and vegetables for *Noodles Parmesan*.

4. Prepare fresh vegetables and nuts at the same time:
   - Chop 1 onion.
   - Chop 1 green pepper.
   - Cut 1 C. broccoli flowers.
   - Chop ½ C. almonds, if needed.
   - Slice 1 C. mushrooms, optional, step 3, p. 69.
   - Chop 1 small zucchini.

5. Use the same fry pan to cook creole vegetables, brown the rice and almonds, and complete *Noodles Parmesan*, washing pan out as needed.

6. Complete each dish in order: creole to cook, pilaf to cook, *Noodles Parmesan*.

7. Place in freezer containers, label, cool in refrigerator if needed, freeze. Include recipe page # on label to refer back to later.

CREOLE PEAS 'N CORN

To thaw and reheat, see p. 8.

1 serving of 6, *includes optional butter (approx. $.60)*
Exchanges: 0.75 meat, 2.25 fat, 3 bread, 2 vegetable
403 calories (302 without the butter)
10.5 grams protein (16%)
12.5 grams fat (27%), 31 mg. cholesterol (Note: Without the butter, only 3% fat!)
60 grams carbohydrate (57%), 12 grams dietary fiber
314 mg. sodium

MENU

868 Calories
21% Fat
$1.35*

CREOLE PEAS 'N CORN (p. 67)

CARROT AND CELERY STICKS

CUCUMBER SLICES

BRAN MUFFINS (p. 168)
WITH JAM

ORANGE AMBROSIA (p. 182)

*For size servings on which data is based, see p. 12. To adjust fat level of menus, see p. 193.

Tasty economical recipe and so easy to make!

1. In large pan, soak peas in water 1 to 3 hours or overnight:

   2 C. (1 lb.) raw black-eyed peas   **8 C. water**

2. Bring peas in water to a boil, add seasonings and boil 3 minutes; reduce heat to simmer:

   1 bay leaf   **$\frac{1}{2}$ tsp. rosemary leaves**
   1 tsp. Italian seasoning   **(crumble between fingers)**

3. In large fry pan sauté vegetables in unsalted butter. Add to simmering peas and continue cooking until peas are almost tender, about 1$\frac{1}{2}$ hours, adding more water, if needed:

   2 tbsp. butter, melted,   **1 green pepper, chopped**
   optional   **1 onion, chopped**

4. Add remaining ingredients, stirring in the corn after completely cooled, just before freezing:

   1 lb. can stewed tomatoes   **2 tbsp. honey**
   8 oz. can tomato sauce   **$\frac{1}{2}$ tsp. salt**
   $\frac{1}{2}$ stick ($\frac{1}{4}$ C.) butter,   **1$\frac{1}{2}$ C. frozen corn**
   optional for added flavor   (most of a 10 oz. package)

5. **To Serve:** Turn frozen out of container into saucepan over direct low heat; add 2 C. water. When completely thawed, bring to a boil, lower to simmering for 30 minutes. Add more water as needed (should be quite soupy). Remove bay leaf before serving.

CHICKEN RICE PILAF

To thaw and reheat, see p. 8.

1 serving of 6, *butter for sautéeing not included (approx. $1.15)*
Exchanges: 2 meat, 0.75 fat, 2.5 bread, 0.75 vegetable
342 calories
28 grams protein (33%)
6.5 grams fat (18%), 58 mg. cholesterol
42 grams carbohydrate (49%), 4 grams dietary fiber
452 mg. sodium

MENU

CHICKEN RICE PILAF *(p. 69)*

**FROZEN OR FRESH GREEN BEANS
OR PEAS**

PINEAPPLE ORANGE GELATIN *(p. 157)*
ON LEAFY LETTUCE

HOT WHOLE GRAIN ROLLS *(p. 162)*
WITH JAM

636 Calories
11% Fat
$1.95*

*For size servings on which data is based, see p. 12. To adjust fat level of menus, see p. 193.

9" x 13" Pan or 2½ Quart Casserole ~ Serves 6

*Our company rice pilaf with chicken added. Especially tasty with **Sue's Kitchen Magic**.*

1. **Optional for Flavor:** In large fry pan lightly brown rice and almonds in unsalted butter over moderately low heat, stirring frequently:

   ½ stick (¼ C.) butter, melted   **¼ C. slivered almonds**
   1½ C. raw long grain brown rice   **(or whole almonds, chopped)**

2. In medium saucepan combine and bring to a boil:

   3 C. water   **2 tsp. Worcestershire**
   4 tsp. *Sue's Kitchen Magic* *(p. 52)*   **or soy sauce** *(p. 94)*

3. Add rice and almonds, boil moderately, uncovered, for 5 minutes; cover tightly, reduce heat to very low, and simmer 45-60 minutes until all water is absorbed and rice is done. Fold in:

   2 C. (1 lb.) cooked chicken, chopped in bite-sized pieces *(p. 145)*
   8 oz. can sliced water chestnuts, drained
   4 oz. can mushrooms, drained, or 1 C. fresh sliced mushrooms

4. **To Serve:** Top with **2 chopped green onions** (lightly sautéed in a little water).

VARIATION: In place of ingredients in step 3, use **3 C. chicken broth, ⅛ tsp. garlic powder, ½ tsp. salt** (if broth is unsalted).

VEGETARIAN ALTERNATIVE: Omit chicken. Use **½ C. almonds**; add lightly sautéed **1 C. chopped celery, 1 diced carrot, 1 C. sliced fresh mushrooms**.

To thaw and reheat, see p. 8.

1 serving of 5, using light sour cream, includes butter (approx. $.85)
   Exchanges: 0.75 meat, 4.5 fat, 2.25 bread, 0.5 vegetable
   416 calories
   16 grams protein (15%)
   22.5 grams fat (48%), 49 mg. cholesterol
   39 grams carbohydrate (37%), 11 grams dietary fiber
   577 mg. sodium

MENU

**743 Calories
36% Fat
$1.55***

NOODLES PARMESAN *(p. 71)*

ARRANGED TOMATO/CUCUMBER SALAD *(p. 158)*
WITH ¼ C. GRATED CARROTS
WITH BASIL AND HERB VINEGAR

BUTTERMILK DROP BISCUITS *(p. 180)*
OR BAKED BROWN BREAD *(p. 169)*
WITH JAM

For size servings on which data is based, see p. 12. To adjust fat level of menus, see p. 193.

About 2 Quart Casserole ~ Serves 4-5

Noodle dishes are especially pleasing when made with Kamut pasta (p. 20).

1. Cook noodles by the standard method *(p. 152)*, adding broccoli and zucchini to cook the last minute:

   8 oz. whole grain noodles *(p. 20)*   **1 C. broccoli flowers**
   1 small zucchini, unpeeled, chopped   (cut quite small)
   (about 1 C.)

2. **Optional for Flavor:** In large fry pan sauté almonds and fresh garlic in unsalted butter:

   ½ stick (¼ C.) butter, melted   **2 cloves garlic, minced**
   ¼ C. almonds, slivered or chopped   **or ¼ tsp. garlic powder**

3. In small mixing bowl whisk together and stir into almonds and garlic:

   1 C. light sour cream or sour cream   **½ tsp. salt, to taste**
   ½ C. Parmesan cheese

4. Fold in drained noodles and vegetables.

5. **To Serve:** Spark up the color with a garnish of **chopped fresh parsley**.

VARIATIONS: This dish lends itself well to a variety of different vegetables. Add as desired: **chopped carrots, celery, chopped green, yellow**, or **red bell pepper** (all lightly steamed or sautéed), **frozen peas, fresh sliced mushrooms**, etc.

SHOPPER'S GUIDE TO...
DAIRY AND CHEESE

MILK: Use lowfat or nonfat. *Lactaid* is lactose reduced. Skip all imitation milks and dairy cream substitutes.

BUTTERMILK: Available at $1/2$%, 1%, 2% fat (equivalent to lowfat). Use the lowest fat available (nutrient data in this book is based on 2% fat). Pint size is often available. Keeps well. *Darigold* powdered buttermilk is available in some health food stores.

YOGURT: Always buy yogurt with active, live, or viable cultures, and preferably with *lactobacillus acidophilus*. Use nonfat in preference to others.

SOUR CREAM: Available fat-free, light (about half the fat), and regular.

CHEESE: Many varieties of reduced fat and sodium are now available, but you can use regular cheddar (try to buy white) in our menus without an undue rise in fat percentage. Mozzarella contains half the fat of cheddar. I use *Suprema* brand of Parmesan cheese which contains no preservatives.

EGGS: I recommend free-range-fed (often labeled *fertile*). These eggs do not contain chemicals fed to chickens and are nutritionally superior. Purchase at health food stores.

FREEZER SET #7

Chicken Soup, p. 77 • Spaghetti-Joe Sauce, p. 79 • Broccoli Rice Casserole, p. 81

MEATS/FISH/POULTRY:
chicken, 1 whole or parts
ground turkey, 1 lb.

DAIRY:
Parmesan cheese, 2 oz. (1/2 C.)
eggs, 4
lowfat milk, 1/2 C.
butter, 1 tbsp.
cheddar or jack cheese, 3 oz. (3/4 C.)

GRAINS/BEANS/PASTAS/NUTS:
almonds, 2 oz. (1/4 C.)
brown rice, 1/2 lb.

STAPLES:
Check for parsley, ketchup, soy sauce.

FRESH PRODUCE:
onions, 2 large, 1 small
celery, 3 ribs plus tops
carrots, 1 lb. (or 5)
broccoli, 12 oz. to 1 lb.
garlic, 3 cloves
fresh parsley

FROZEN:
frozen peas, 5 oz. (1 C.)

CANNED FOODS/MISCELLANEOUS:
whole tomatoes, 2—14.5 oz. cans
    or tomato sauce, 3—8 oz. cans
tomato paste, 6 oz. can

SEASONINGS/HERBS:
Check *Herb and Spice Cupboard (p. 5)*
against recipes.

73

SHOPPER'S GUIDE TO...
HAMBURGER AND HOT DOG BUNS

YOUR LOCAL HEALTH FOOD STORE IS THE BEST PLACE TO FIND THESE!

The same ingredient standards apply to hamburger and hot dog buns as other whole grain breads (see p. 164). Always read ingredient labels wherever you find them.

Of all the whole grain breads, hamburger and hot dog buns are the most difficult to find. Supermarkets seldom have them. *Roman Meal* brand is about the best available in some supermarkets. Only a few health food stores stock them on a regular basis. If you find them, buy a few packages to put in the freezer. I usually repackage them for the freezer, dividing up the number I want in each package. I wrap them snuggly in plastic wrap, then foil, using them within 2 or 3 months.

Your own buns can be made from any whole grain yeast bread dough. Just shape them accordingly.

CHICKEN SOUP, *p. 77*
SPAGHETTI-JOE SAUCE, *p. 79*
BROCCOLI RICE CASSEROLE, *p. 81*

1. Cook broth and chicken for soup the day or night before; refrigerate.

2. Assemble ingredients for recipes on trays. Get out: 1 large fry pan, large pot for soup, 2 saucepans to cook broccoli and rice (one with tight-fitting lid), a large mixing bowl to mix ground turkey with seasonings and to assemble rice casserole, ovenproof casserole dish for rice casserole, freezer containers.

3. Start rice (cook enough for soup and rice casserole). Heat broth for soup. Season turkey and begin to brown in large fry pan. Heat broccoli water.

4. Prepare fresh vegetables at the same time:
   - Chop 2 large onions.
   - Chop 1 green pepper.
   - Chop 4-5 C. broccoli.
   - Slice 3 carrots.
   - Chop 3 ribs celery.
   - Mince 3 cloves garlic.
   - Chop $1/4$ C. almonds, if needed.

5. Use the same fry pan to complete *Spaghetti-Joe Sauce*, sauté almonds and onions for rice, washing pan out as needed.

6. Complete each dish in order: soup for cooking, *Spaghetti-Joe Sauce*, broccoli rice for baking.

7. Place in freezer containers, label, cool in refrigerator if needed, freeze. Include recipe page # on label to refer back to later.

CHICKEN SOUP

To thaw and reheat, see p. 8.

1 serving of 8 (1½-2 C.), *using 2 qts. broth, 1½ C. cooked rice, 1 C. chicken (approx. $.35)*
  Exchanges: 0.75 meat, 0.75 bread, 1 vegetable
  135 calories
  10 grams protein (27%)
  2.5 grams fat (16%), 15 mg. cholesterol
  20 grams carbohydrate (56%), 3.5 grams dietary fiber
  343 mg. sodium

MENU

607 Calories
29% Fat
$1.00*

CHICKEN SOUP (p. 77)
WITH SOUP 'N SALAD CROUTONS (p. 175)

CABBAGE-PINEAPPLE SALAD (p. 158)
WITH SWEET MAYONNAISE DRESSING (p. 160)

LEMON GINGER MUFFINS (p. 172)
WITH BUTTER SPREAD (p. 171)

*For size servings on which data is based, see p. 12. To adjust fat level of menus, see p. 193.

A great soup to make while stewing chicken for use in recipes or with the leftover chicken bones with bits of chicken. Freeze broth and chicken separately to make soup later, or make and freeze completed soup. Can also be made in a crockpot.

1. Make *Chicken and Broth,* p. 145, by the slow-cooking method to yield at least 1¹/₂-2 qts. broth and 1 or 2 C. bits of cooked chicken.

2. Bring broth to boil in large saucepan, add vegetables, reduce heat to simmer, and cook until vegetables are barely tender, about 30 minutes:

   1 large onion, chopped   **3 carrots, sliced**
   3 ribs celery, chopped   **2 cloves garlic, minced**

3. Add:

   1-1¹/₂ C. cooked rice   **bits of cooked chicken**

4. **To Serve:** Just before serving, add to hot soup and simmer briefly:

   ¹/₂ C. finely chopped fresh parsley   **1 tsp. dill weed**
   1 C. frozen peas   **salt and pepper, to taste**
   Spike seasoning, to taste, optional

VARIATIONS: For added flavor: Sauté vegetables in **2-3 tbsp. melted butter. For a creamy soup:** In separate pan whisk **¹/₂ C. whole wheat pastry or unbleached white flour** into **2 C. lowfat or nonfat milk**. Stir over moderate heat until thickened. Blend into hot soup.

ᔆᕈᗩGHETTI JOE ᔆᗩUCE

To thaw and reheat, see p. 8.

1 serving of 6 (about 1 C.), *using 90% fat-free ground turkey (approx. $.85)*
    Exchanges: 2.5 meat, 3 vegetable
    228 calories
    24 grams protein (40%)
    8.5 grams fat (31%), 48 mg. cholesterol
    18 grams carbohydrate (29%), 2.5 grams dietary fiber
    596 mg. sodium

MENU

642 Calories
28% Fat
$1.90*

SPAGHETTI-JOE SAUCE (p. 79)
OVER SPAGHETTI (p. 152)
OR TOASTED HAMBURGER BUN HALVES (p. 74)
WITH 1 TBSP. PARMESAN CHEESE

FROZEN CORN

TOSSED SALAD (p. 158)
WITH NEWMAN'S OWN DRESSING

*For size servings on which data is based, see p. 12. To adjust fat level of menus, see p. 193.

SPAGHETTI JOE SAUCE

About 1½ Quarts ~ Serves 6-8

A family favorite to serve with whole grain spaghetti or whole grain buns for sloppy joes.

1. In large fry pan brown the turkey, adding onion and green pepper the last 5 minutes:

   1 lb. *Seasoned Ground Turkey* (p. 149)
   ½ large or 1 small onion, chopped
   1 small green pepper, chopped

2. Blend in:

   2—14.5 oz. cans whole tomatoes, no salt added (p. 94)
      or 3—8 oz. cans tomato sauce, no salt added
      or 2—1 lb. cans stewed tomatoes
   6 oz. can tomato paste
   1 tsp. soy sauce (p. 94)
   1¼ tsp. oregano leaves
   1¼ tsp. sweet basil leaves
   ¼ tsp. thyme leaves
   ⅛ tsp. garlic powder

3. **To Serve:** Simmer 30 minutes to blend flavors.

VEGETARIAN ALTERNATIVE: Omit ground turkey. If desired, add **2 C. cooked lentils, kidney beans,** or **tofu cubes.**

BROCCOLI RICE CASSEROLE

To thaw and reheat, see p. 8.

1 serving of 6 *(approx. $.70)*
Exchanges: 2 meat, 1.5 fat, 2 bread, 1 vegetable
353 calories
18.5 grams protein (20%)
17.5 grams fat (45%), 171 mg. cholesterol
38.5 grams carbohydrate (42%), 6 grams dietary fiber
628 mg. sodium

MENU

**722 Calories
27% Fat
$1.40***

BROCCOLI RICE CASSEROLE *(p. 81)*

ARRANGED TOMATO/CUCUMBER SALAD *(p. 158)*
WITH JULIENNE CARROT STICKS
WITH DILL WEED AND HERB VINEGAR

BRAN MUFFINS *(p. 168)*
OR BAKED BROWN BREAD OR HOT ROLLS
WITH JAM

*For size servings on which data is based, see p. 12. To adjust fat level of menus, see p. 193.

Serves 6

A very satisfying, colorful, and tasty casserole.

Bake: 350° for 20-25 min., covered (2-2¹/₂ qt. ovenproof casserole)

1. Cook a recipe of *Brown Rice* (p. 148).

2. Cook broccoli (p. 156) and drain:

    4-5 C. fresh broccoli, chopped small (use both stems and flowers)

3. In large fry pan sauté onion, garlic, almonds in unsalted butter:

    1 tbsp. melted butter   **¹/₂ large or ¹/₂ C. chopped onion**
    1 clove garlic, minced   **¹/₄ C. chopped or slivered almonds**

4. In large mixing bowl mix together:

    4 eggs, slightly beaten   **sautéed onions, almonds, garlic**
    ¹/₂ C. lowfat milk   **cooked broccoli**
    ¹/₂ C. Parmesan cheese   **cooked rice**
    ¹/₈ tsp. nutmeg

5. Place in lightly sprayed or buttered casserole dish, cover, and bake.

6. **To Serve:** Top completely thawed casserole just before heating with:

    ³/₄ C. grated cheddar or jack cheese
    paprika
    fresh chopped or dried parsley flakes or chives

81

FRANKS: Franks of nutritionally high quality in supermarkets are a rarity. They typically contain pork, dextrose, sodium nitrate or nitrite, and other unpronounceable ingredients. I recommend *Health Valley* brand chicken franks, available in some health food stores, which contain no questionable ingredients and have a good flavor. They are high in sodium, though, so use them judiciously. Other brands are also available. *Health Valley* produces meatless franks from tofu which are quite good as well.

TOFU: Tofu is readily available at supermarkets in 10 oz., 14 oz., or 16 oz. packaging. Tofu made from organic soybeans is available in health food stores. Special packaging for long-term storage (as long as a year) is a good buy. It can be kept in a cool dry place until opened or in the refrigerator. *Mori-Nu* and *Kikkoman* are two brands packaged for long-term storage.

FREEZER SET #8

• *Chili Gourmet, p. 87* • *Macaroni 'n Cheese, p. 89* • *Barbecue Franks 'n Beans, p. 91*

MEATS/FISH/POULTRY:
ground turkey, 1 lb.
chicken franks, 1 pkg.

DAIRY:
lowfat milk, 1½ C.
cheddar cheese, ½ lb. (2 C.)
butter, ½ stick (¼ C.)

FROZEN:
green beans, 10 oz.
green lima beans, 10 oz.
corn, 10 oz.

FRESH PRODUCE:
onions, 2
green pepper, 1 large
mushrooms, ⅓ lb. (2 C.)
garlic, 2 cloves

GRAINS/BEANS/PASTAS/NUTS:
*whole grain macaroni, 8 oz.
*whole wheat pastry flour, ¼ C.
*whole grain bread, 2 slices

CANNED FOODS/MISCELLANEOUS:
kidney beans, 15 oz. can
kidney beans, 27 oz. can
tomato pieces, 2—16 oz. cans

STAPLES:
Check for ketchup, apple cider vinegar,
Tabasco sauce, Worcestershire sauce,
honey, mustard, parsley.

SEASONINGS/HERBS:
Check *Herb and Spice Cupboard* (p. 5)
against recipes.

*It may be necessary to purchase these items at a health food store.

Let's Talk Tofu!

- Made from soybeans
- Most easily digestible form of soybeans
- High protein—16 grams per cup (44%)
- Complements grain protein
- No cholesterol
- Good source of linoleic acid (an essential fatty acid)
- Tasteless: adaptable to many flavors
- A vegetarian alternative to meat in many recipes
- Easy to use
- Easy to find (p. 82)
- Long-term storage available (p. 82)
- Inexpensive

84

ASSEMBLY TIPS

CHILI GOURMET, *p. 87*
MACARONI 'N CHEESE, *p. 89*
BARBECUE FRANKS 'N BEANS, *p. 91*

1. Assemble ingredients for recipes on trays. Get out: 1 large fry pan, large pan to cook pasta and assemble chili, medium saucepan for cheese sauce, large mixing bowl for seasoning ground turkey and assembling macaroni dish, ovenproof casserole for macaroni 'n cheese, freezer containers.

2. Start water heating for macaroni, season ground turkey and start to brown.

3. Prepare fresh vegetables, cheese, franks at the same time:
   - Chop 1 green pepper.
   - Slice 2 C. mushrooms.
   - Chop 2 onions.
   - Diagonally slice franks in bite-size pieces.
   - Grate 2 C. cheddar cheese.

4. Use the same fry pan to cook turkey and vegetables for chili, to brown franks and assemble barbecue beans 'n franks, washing pan out as needed. Use same pot to cook macaroni and assemble chili.

5. Complete each dish in order: *Chili Gourmet, Barbecue Franks 'n Beans, Macaroni 'n Cheese.*

6. Place in freezer containers, label, cool in refrigerator if needed, freeze. Include recipe page # on label to refer back to later.

CHILI GOURMET

To thaw and reheat, see p. 8.

About 1 C. serving, *using 90% fat-free ground turkey (approx. $.70)*
 Exchanges: 1.75 meat, 1.25 bread, 1.5 vegetable
 223 calories
 19 grams protein (34%)
 5 grams fat (20%), 29 mg. cholesterol
 26 grams carbohydrate (46%), 4.5 grams dietary fiber
 569 mg. sodium

MENU

699 Calories
28% Fat
$1.55*

1¹/₂ C. CHILI GOURMET *(p. 87)*

2 PIECES CORNBREAD *(p. 178)*
WITH HONEY BUTTER SPREAD *(p. 173)*

CARROT STICKS

TOSSED GREENS
WITH 1¹/₂ TSP. PARMESAN CHEESE
AND LEMON-OLIVE OIL DRESSING *(p. 161)*

*For size servings on which data is based, see p. 12. To adjust fat level of menus, see p. 193.

10 Cups or 1¹/₂ Quart Casserole ~ Serves 6-8

With or without ground turkey, the pepper and mushrooms give a special touch to this dish.

1. Season turkey and brown in large fry pan, adding vegetables about the last 5 minutes:

   1 lb. *Seasoned Ground Turkey* (p. 149)   **1 large green pepper, chopped**
   1 onion, chopped   **2 C. sliced fresh mushrooms**

2. Meanwhile, in large 3 qt. pot combine and heat until hot:

   15 oz. plus 27 oz. can kidney beans,   **2 cloves minced garlic**
      drained, rinsed*   **1 tbsp. chili powder**
   1¹/₂ C. water (or bean juice, if desired)   **1¹/₂ tsp. cumin powder**
   2—16 oz. cans tomato pieces   **1 tsp. salt, to taste**

3. Blend in cooked ground turkey and vegetables.

4. **To Serve:** To thawed casserole in pot, add water, if needed, to just cover ingredients, bring just to a boil, reduce to simmer, and cook briefly, about 10 minutes.

*Thorough rinsing will remove up to 40% of the sodium. If desired, in place of canned beans, crockpot cook 2 C. dry kidney beans (p. 147).

VEGETARIAN ALTERNATIVE: Omit ground turkey. If desired add **1 block tofu**, pre-frozen, crumbled (drain block; cover with fresh water; freeze overnight; press out moisture and crumble under hot running water).

To thaw and reheat, see p. 8.

1 serving of 6, *includes buttered bread crumbs (approx. $.55)*
  Exchanges: 2.5 meat, 0.25 milk, 1.5 fat, 2.5 bread
  404 calories
  19 grams protein (19%)
  21 grams fat (46%), 61 mg. cholesterol
  36.5 grams carbohydrate (35%), 8.5 grams dietary fiber
  358 mg. sodium

MENU

643 Calories
35% Fat
$1.55*

MACARONI 'N CHEESE (p. 89)

**FROZEN OR FRESH GREEN BEANS,
PEAS, OR CARROTS**

TOSSED SALAD (p. 158)
WITH SWEET ORANGE DRESSING (p. 160)
OR HERB VINEGAR

APPLE

*For size servings on which data is based, see p. 12. To adjust fat level of menus, see p. 193.

Serves 4-6

A healthier and tasty version of an old-time family favorite! We prefer the taste and texture of Kamut macaroni or macaroni made with unbleached durum spring wheat and soy or sesame rather than whole wheat macaroni for this recipe (see p. 20).

Bake: 350° for 30 minutes, uncovered (2-2¹/₂ qt. ovenproof casserole)

1. Cook and drain macaroni (p. 152):

   8 oz. (2 C. raw) whole grain macaroni (p. 20)

2. **Cheese sauce:** In medium saucepan melt butter, blend in flour, cooking 1 minute; remove from heat and whisk in milk; cook and stir over moderate heat until thickened; stir in salt and cheese to melt:

   3 tbsp. unsalted butter **2 C. grated cheddar cheese**
   4¹/₂ tbsp. whole wheat pastry flour **¹/₄ tsp. salt, to taste**
   (or ¹/₄ C. unbleached white flour)
   1¹/₂ C. lowfat milk

3. In a large bowl combine cooked macaroni with cheese sauce.

4. Place in casserole dish and bake.

5. **To Serve:** While reheating thawed covered casserole, uncover the last 10 minutes and top with ***Buttered Bread Crumbs*** (blend bread and parsley in blender; combine with butter in small bowl):

   2 slices soft whole grain bread, broken in pieces
   sprig of fresh parsley
   1 tbsp. unsalted butter, melted

❧ BARBECUE FRANKS 'N BEANS ❧

To thaw and reheat, see p. 8.

1 serving of 5 *(approx. $1.30)*
Exchanges: 3.75 meat, 1.5 fat, .75 bread, 3.75 vegetable
446 calories
19 grams protein (16%)
24 grams fat (46%), 90 mg. cholesterol
43 grams carbohydrate (37%), 9 grams dietary fiber
1,771 mg. sodium

MENU

815 Calories
28% Fat
$1.90*

BARBECUE FRANKS 'N BEANS *(p. 91)*

CABBAGE-CARROT SALAD *(p. 158)*
WITH SWEET LITE DRESSING *(p. 160)*

BAKED BROWN BREAD *(p. 169)*

FRESH PINEAPPLE WEDGES *(p. 92)*

For size servings on which data is based, see p. 12. To adjust fat level of menus, see p. 193.

1½ Quart Casserole ~ Serves 4-5

For frank lovers. Use half package of franks to cut sodium and fat, if desired (each frank contains 616 mg. sodium). Serve with lots of lowfat accompaniments.

1. Cut franks diagonally in bite-sized pieces and brown lightly and evenly in oil in large fry pan; remove from pan:

   10 oz. package chicken franks *(p. 82)*　　　**2 tbsp. olive oil** *(p. 171)*

2. In same pan sauté onion in a little water (or additional oil); blend in remaining ingredients just to warm:

   1 onion, chopped　　　　　　　　　**½ tsp. pepper**
   ½ C. water　　　　　　　　　　　　**¼ tsp. Tabasco sauce**
   ½ C. ketchup *(p. 94)*　　　　　　　**1 tsp. salt**
   ¼ C. apple cider vinegar　　　　　　**1 tsp. paprika**
   1 tbsp. Worcestershire sauce *(p. 94)*　**1 tsp. mustard** *(p. 94)*
   1 tbsp. honey

3. Break up and combine with franks and sauce (keeping as unthawed as possible), 10 oz. frozen package each:

   10 oz. pkg. (2 C.) green beans　　　**10 oz. pkg. (2 C.) corn**
   10 oz. pkg. (2 C.) green lima beans

4. **To Serve:** Simmer thawed dish 15 minutes, adding a little water, if needed.

VEGETARIAN ALTERNATIVE: Omit chicken franks. Add **meatless franks**, *Health Valley* brand made from tofu *(p. 82)*.

91

Pineapple Pointers

*S*erve pineapple often! It adds a delicious complementary taste and texture to many meals. Pineapple also contains the enzyme bromelin which helps to digest protein.

To Peel and Cut:
- *Slice off top and bottom.*
- *Stand on end and cut in fourths lengthwise.*
- *Cut each fourth lengthwise in half or thirds.*
- *Stand wedge on peel and cut away from peel (a curved boning knife works great!).*
- *Cut off tough center strip from wedge.*
- *Cut desired size wedges or chunks.*

FREEZER SET #9
• *Split Pea Soup, p. 97* • *Meat Loaf, p. 99* • *Enchilada Casserole, p. 101*

MEATS/FISH/POULTRY:
ground turkey, 2 lbs.

DAIRY:
eggs, 2 medium
cheddar cheese, 6 oz. (1½ C.)
Parmesan cheese, optional,
   see step 5, p. 97

FRESH PRODUCE:
onions, 3
carrots, 3
celery, 3 ribs or leaves

STAPLES:
Check for ketchup, soy sauce.

GRAINS/BEANS/PASTAS/NUTS:
*stoneground tortillas, 6
 split peas, 1 lb. (2 C.)
 rolled oats, old fashioned, ½ C.

CANNED FOODS/MISCELLANEOUS:
*enchilada or *pasta sauce,
     16-24 oz. (2-3 C.) or 1 qt.,
     see step 5, p. 101
tomato sauce, 8 oz. can
sliced ripe olives, 2 oz. can
diced green chiles, 4 oz. can

SEASONINGS/HERBS:
Check *Herb and Spice Cupboard*
(p. 5) against recipes.

It may be necessary to purchase these items at a health food store.

93

• *tomatoes* • *tomato sauce* • *tomato paste* • *pasta/spaghetti sauce* • *ketchup*
• *Worcestershire sauce* • *soy sauce* • *mustard* • *mayonnaise* • *pickle relish* • *jam*

Ingredients to minimize: salt, refined sugar, distilled vinegar, EDTA, emulsifiers

EXEMPLARY QUALITY BRANDS

- tomato products: salt-reduced or no salt, such as *Hunts*

- pasta/spaghetti sauces: *Ragu* (salt-reduced); *Enrico, Health Valley, Westbrae, Johnson's* (health food stores)

- *Featherweight* ketchup, mustard (no salt)

- *Hollywoood* mayonnaise, *Hain* mayonnaise (health food stores)

- *Kikkoman Lite* soy sauce (reduced sodium)

- *Robbie's* or *Lite All Natural* Worcestershire sauce (health food stores)

- pickle relish: honey sweetened; *Cascadian Farms* (health food stores)

- jam: all fruit, honey sweetened, or low sugar

SPLIT PEA SOUP, *p. 97*
MEAT LOAF, *p. 99*
ENCHILADA CASSEROLE, *p. 101*

1. Separate tortillas for enchilada casserole and freeze overnight.

2. Assemble ingredients for recipes on trays. Get out: 1 large fry pan, large pot for soup, 1 medium mixing bowl for seasoning turkey and mixing meat loaf, medium loaf pan for meat loaf, ovenproof casserole for enchilada casserole, freezer container for soup.

3. Start peas cooking for soup. In medium mixing bowl season ground turkey and start browning for enchilada casserole. Use same bowl later to mix meat loaf.

4. Prepare fresh vegetables and cheese at the same time:
   - Chop 2 onions plus ½ C.
   - Dice or slice 3 carrots.
   - Chop 3 ribs celery or bunch celery leaves.
   - Grate 1½ C. cheddar cheese.

5. Complete each dish in order: meat loaf for baking, enchilada casserole, soup.

6. Freeze enchilada casserole immediately. Cool soup in the pot and put into freezer container, label and freeze. Cool meat loaf in pan in refrigerator, wrap, label, and freeze. Include recipe page # on labels to refer back to later.

SPLIT PEA SOUP

To thaw and reheat, see p. 8.

1 serving of 4, *salt and garnishes not included (approx. $.35)*
  Exchanges: 1.5 meat, 3.5 bread, 2 vegetable
  399 calories
  26 grams protein (25%)
  2 grams fat (4%), 0 mg. cholesterol
  74.5 grams carbohydrate (71%), 20.5 grams dietary fiber
  110 mg. sodium

MENU

774 Calories
8% Fat
$1.35*

SPLIT PEA SOUP *(p. 97)*
WITH SOUP 'N SALAD CROUTONS *(p. 175)*

ARRANGED TOMATO/CUCUMBER SALAD *(p. 158)*
WITH 1/4 C. COTTAGE CHEESE/YOGURT
OR HERB VINEGAR

ORANGE OR BRAN MUFFINS *(pp. 168, 170)*

For size servings on which data is based, see p. 12. To adjust fat level of menus, see p. 193.

SPLIT PEA SOUP

Serves 4-6

Surprisingly tasty without hambone. May be crockpot cooked as well, combining all ingredients at once except salt in pot to cook overnight on low or 5 to 6 hours on high.

1. Bring peas and water to a boil; boil 3 minutes; reduce heat to very gentle boil until peas are tender, 45-60 minutes, adding more water, if needed:

   2 C. dry green split peas   **8 C. water**

2. Add and continue very gentle boil until vegetables are tender, about 15-25 minutes, adding more water, if needed:

   1 onion, chopped   **3 ribs celery, chopped**
   3 carrots, diced or sliced   **or chopped leaves**
   1 bay leaf

3. Season with salt, to taste. I have also used 4 tsp. *Sue's Kitchen Magic* (p. 52) in place of salt. We like it, although the taste is a little different.

4. Remove bay leaf. **Optional:** Puree part or all of soup in blender, as desired. Blending helps to thicken soup and increase flavor.

5. **To Serve:** Garnish hot soup, as desired, with:

   Parmesan cheese   *Soup 'n Salad Croutons* (p. 175)
   Spike seasoning (p. 5)

VARIATIONS: To thawed hot soup add **1-2 C. cooked potato chunks** or **1 C. cooked brown rice** or **barley** (the latter two may be added before freezing).

1 serving of 8, *using 90% fat-free ground turkey (approx. $.50)*
Exchanges: 3 meat, 0.5 bread, 0.25 fat, 0.5 vegetable
229 calories
27 grams protein (46%)
10 grams fat (39%), 109 mg. cholesterol
9 grams carbohydrate (15%), 1 gram dietary fiber
617 mg. sodium

MENU

569 Calories
32% Fat
$1.50*

MEAT LOAF (p. 99) WITH 2 TBSP. KETCHUP

6 OZ. BAKED POTATO (p. 137)
WITH LIGHT SOUR CREAM/NONFAT YOGURT (2 TBSP. EACH)

FROZEN OR FRESH GREEN BEANS, PEAS, OR CARROTS

ORANGE-LETTUCE-BANANA SALAD (p. 158)
WITH SWEET MAYONNAISE DRESSING (p. 160)

*For size servings on which data is based, see p. 12. To adjust fat level of menus, see p. 193.

Tasty traditional meat loaf with ground turkey. I divide this in half after baking for 2 meals.

Bake: 350° for 1-1¼ hours, uncovered (9" x 5" large loaf pan or 9" square pan)

1. In medium mixing bowl blend ingredients together in order given:

   8 oz. (1 C.) tomato sauce   **⅛ -¼ tsp. garlic powder**
   ¾ C. old fashioned rolled oats, uncooked   **½ tsp. salt**
   2 medium eggs or 3 egg whites   **1½ tsp. soy sauce** *(p. 94)*
   ½ C. chopped onion   **1 lb. ground turkey** *(p. 42)*
   1½ tsp. celery salt

2. Pat mixture firmly into large loaf pan, or make a round mounded loaf in 9" square bake pan.

3. Bake. Cool in refrigerator.

4. **To Freeze:** Turn out of pan. Cut loaf in half, if desired, for 2 meals. Wrap securely in plastic wrap, then snuggly in foil.

5. **To Serve:** Cut thawed or partially thawed loaf into serving slices; overlap in baking pan, cover tightly and heat in oven at 350°, about 15 minutes.

VARIATION: In place of salt and soy sauce add **1 tbsp.** *Sue's Kitchen Magic* *(p. 52)*.

To thaw and reheat, see p. 8.

1 serving of 5, using 90% fat-free ground turkey (approx. $1.45)
Exchanges: 2 meat, 4.25 fat, 1 bread, 2.5 vegetable
432 calories
31 grams protein (28%)
21 grams fat, 88 mg. cholesterol
33 grams carbohydrate (29%), 6.5 grams dietary fiber
675 mg. sodium

MENU

644 Calories
30% Fat
$1.95*

ENCHILADA CASSEROLE (p. 101)

ARRANGED ORANGE/PINEAPPLE SALAD (p. 158)
WITH SWEET LITE DRESSING (p. 160)

FANTASTIC BROCCOLI (p. 156)

LITE CHOCOLATE PUDDING (p. 186)

For size servings on which data is based, see p. 12. To adjust fat level of menus, see p. 193.

2 Quart Casserole ~ Serves 4-5

An easy way to make enchiladas! For heating in a conventional oven, prepare this dish in an oven-proof casserole since it cannot be easily transferred to another container once made.

1. Separate and freeze the tortillas overnight to prevent softening and breaking when the dish is frozen and thawed.

2. Season turkey and brown in large fry pan adding onion, drained chilies, and olives the last 5 minutes of cooking:

   1 lb. *Seasoned Ground Turkey* (p. 149)   **4 oz. can diced green chilies**
   1 onion, chopped   **2¼ oz. can sliced ripe olives, drained**

3. In an ovenproof casserole dish about the same diameter as the tortillas (not a must, but helps), layer alternately in order given, starting and ending with a layer of sauce on bottom and top of dish:

   6 stoneground corn tortillas (p. 177)   **1½ C. grated cheddar cheese**
   2-3 C. pasta or enchilada sauce (p. 94)   **cooked ground turkey mixture**

4. Freeze casserole immediately.

5. **To Serve:** Reheat in conventional oven. Add more enchilada sauce* if a little dry. Uncover for last 15-20 minutes.

*If desired, freeze leftover sauce separately to unthaw and add to casserole later.

VEGETARIAN ALTERNATIVE: Omit ground turkey. Add **15 oz. can (drained) or 2 C. crockpot pinto beans, black beans, or kidney beans** (p. 147).

Vegetarian Alternatives

*T*ry these ideas for meat replacements. We've used them all in 26 of the main dish recipes in this book:

- Add cooked lentils or kidney beans.

- Add nuts, especially cashews or almonds.

- Add sliced fresh mushrooms.

- Increase the vegetables, or add extra ones.

- Add tofu cubes or tofu products such as meatless franks.

- Use *Sue's Kitchen Magic* (p. 52) with water in place of chicken or beef broth (about 1 tsp. to 1 C. water).

Crockpot and Quick Meals

Enjoy quick-fix dinners alternately with frozen main dishes! Use the freezer to speed preparation of these meals. Some of the crockpot dishes may be frozen. Other things to do ahead:

- Season, brown, and freeze extra *Seasoned Ground Turkey* (p. 149) to have on hand for such dishes as *Ragout* and *Taco Chip Olé*.

- Season, shape, and freeze turkey burger patties for *Turkey Burgers* (p. 113).

- Cook *Chicken and Broth* (p. 145); freeze for such dishes as *Javanese Dinner* (p. 119).

- Grate cheddar cheese for several dishes and freeze in suitable sized packages.

- Stock cupboard ahead with nonperishable ingredients for quick meals.

- Keep *Basic Stock* (staples, refrigerated and frozen perishables) and *Herb and Spice Cupboard* updated (pp. 2-5) .

CROCKPOT STEW

1 C. serving *(approx. $.95)*
Exchanges: 3.5 meat, 2 bread, 2 vegetable
371 calories
19.5 grams protein (21%)
16.5 grams fat (40%), 54 mg. cholesterol
37 grams carbohydrate (39%), 10.5 grams dietary fiber
521 mg. sodium

MENU

732 Calories
29% Fat
$1.45*

CROCKPOT STEW *(p. 105)*

CABBAGE-PINEAPPLE SALAD *(p. 158)*
WITH SWEET LITE DRESSING *(p. 160)*

BUTTERMILK DROP BISCUITS *(p. 180)*
WITH JAM

OR SOURDOUGH BREAD *(p. 164)*
WITH BUTTER SPREAD *(p. 171)*

*For size servings on which data is based, see p. 12. To adjust fat level of menus, see p. 193.

12 Cups ~ Serves 6-8

Beef stew lends itself well to crockpot cookery. Pre-browning the stew meat isn't essential when crockpotting, but facilitates removal of fat. Potatoes don't freeze well, so leave them out to add later if you freeze this dish.

Crockpot: 10-12 hours low, or 6 hours high

1. Trim as much fat as possible from meat, cut into small pieces, and brown (optional) in fry pan; drain well and place in crockpot; add remaining ingredients, cover, and cook:

1½ lbs. beef stew meat	5 medium potatoes, cut in small pieces
4 C. water or beef broth	6 carrots, cut in small chunks
¼ C. minute tapioca (thickens stew)	2 onions, coarsely chopped
2 cloves minced garlic	3 ribs celery, sliced on diagonal
1 tsp. paprika	1 rutabaga, cut in small chunks, optional
2 tsp. Worcestershire sauce	2 bay leaves
1½ tbsp. *Sue's Kitchen Magic** (p. 52)	

2. A few minutes before serving stir in:

   10 oz. package or 1½ C. frozen peas
   salt, to taste, optional

*Use **Sue's Kitchen Magic** with water or beef broth.*

VEGETARIAN ALTERNATIVE: Omit beef. Add **1-1½ C. dry lentils or kidney beans,** or add with frozen peas **1 package drained, cubed tofu.**

CROCKPOT O' LIMAS

To thaw and reheat, see p. 8.

1½ C. serving, using *canned beans (reduce sodium by cooking dry beans) (approx. $1.35)*
    Exchanges: 0.75 meat, 0.75 fat, 3.75 vegetable
    386 calories
    16 grams protein (16%)
    6 grams fat (13%), 0 mg. cholesterol
    73 grams carbohydrate (71%), 16.5 grams dietary fiber
    1,218 mg. sodium (reduce 40% by thoroughly rinsing beans 1 minute under running water)

MENU

812 Calories
23% Fat
$1.90*

CROCKPOT O' LIMAS *(p. 107)*

ORANGE-LETTUCE-BANANA SALAD *(p. 158)*
WITH SWEET MAYONNAISE DRESSING *(p. 160)*

BRAN MUFFINS *(p. 168)*
OR BAKED BROWN BREAD *(p. 169)*
WITH TANGY SPREAD *(p. 173)*

For size servings on which data is based, see p. 12. To adjust fat level of menus, see p. 193.

5 Cups ~ Serves 4

An uncomplicated family bean stew. Especially easy to make with precooked beans (p. 147). Very high fiber and low fat! This may be frozen.

Crockpot: Overnight and then some on low or half the time on high

1. Put in the crockpot to cook overnight *(p. 147)*:

2 C. dry lima beans	**5-6 C. water**
1 onion, chopped	**5 cloves garlic, minced**
1 green pepper, minced	

2. When beans are tender, drain well, add and cook to blend flavors:

2—14.5 oz. cans whole tomatoes, no salt added *(p. 94)*	**1 tsp. Italian seasoning**
10 oz. pkg. (2 C.) frozen corn	**1 tsp. salt**
1 tbsp. lemon juice	**¹/₂ tsp. rosemary leaves**
1 tbsp. honey	**1 bay leaf**

3. Just before serving remove bay leaf and stir in:

   ¹/₄ C. minced fresh or 1 tbsp. dried parsley

VARIATIONS:

• Omit step 1. In place of dry beans use **2—15 oz. cans butter beans** (drained, well rinsed); crockpot on low to blend flavors well.

• For added flavor, sauté onion, garlic, green pepper in **1 tbsp. olive oil** and add with ingredients in step 2 instead of adding to dry beans.

To thaw and reheat, see p. 8.

***About 1¹/₂ C.**, excluding butter and salt (approx. $.40)*
  Exchanges: 0.25 bread, 2.25 vegetable
  70 calories
  2.5 grams protein (13%)
  0.1 gram fat (1%), 0 mg. cholesterol
  16.5 grams carbohydrate (86%), 4 grams dietary fiber
  321 mg. sodium

MENU

519 Calories
13% Fat
$1.40*

CROCKPOT GARDEN SOUP *(p. 109)*
WITH SOUP 'N SALAD CROUTONS *(p. 175)*

ARRANGED ORANGE/PINEAPPLE SALAD *(p. 158)*
WITH ¹/₂ C. COTTAGE CHEESE/YOGURT
OR SWEET MAYONNAISE DRESSING *(p. 160)*

LEMON GINGER MUFFINS *(p. 172)*

For size servings on which data is based, see p. 12. To adjust fat level of menus, see p. 193.

CROCKPOT GARDEN SOUP

5-6 Quarts ~ Serves 15

Our favorite company soup for first course and frequent family main course. This freezes well. For freezing, cook vegetables on the light side and add cooked potatoes with the beans and zucchini.

Crockpot: Overnight or 6-8 hours on low, 3-4 hours on high

1. Optional for added flavor, sauté vegetables lightly in butter:

    ¼ C. unsalted butter, melted   **2 C. chopped celery**
    1 large onion, chopped   **2 cloves garlic, minced**

2. Add sautéed vegetables and remaining ingredients to crockpot and cook until vegetables are tender:

    6 C. water   **2 C. thin carrot rounds**
    2—28 oz. cans tomatoes   **2 C. diced raw potatoes**
    1-2 tbsp. *Sue's Kitchen Magic* *(p. 52)*

3. Add about 30 minutes before serving:

    10 oz. (2 C.) frozen green beans,   **1-2 small zucchini, sliced**
    French cut, whole, or cut   **½ C. minced fresh parsley**

4. Adjust seasoning, to taste.

VARIATION: Add as desired **broccoli flowers, cauliflowerets, diced patty pan squash, green pepper, shredded cabbage or spinach, corn, frozen peas;** add later in cooking process so as not to overcook and lose color.

109

To thaw and reheat, see p. 8.

1 serving of 8—about 1¹/₂-2 C., *excluding chicken or turkey (approx. $.40)*
  Exchanges: 0.75 meat, 2 bread, 1 vegetable
  216 calories
  14 grams protein (25%)
  1 gram fat (5%), 0 mg. cholesterol
  39.5 grams carbohydrate (70%), 11 grams dietary fiber
  108 mg. sodium

MENU

736 Calories
27% Fat
$1.20*

NAVY 'N GREEN BEAN SOUP *(p. 111)*
WITH SOUP 'N SALAD CROUTONS *(p. 175)*

CARROT-RAISIN SALAD *(p. 158)*
WITH SWEET MAYONNAISE DRESSING *(p. 160)*

2 WHOLE WHEAT TORTILLAS *(p. 164)*
WITH TANGY SPREAD *(p. 173)*

For size servings on which data is based, see p. 12. To adjust fat level of menus, see p. 193.

Serves 8

A tasty change-of-pace soup with green beans. This dish may be frozen.

Crockpot: Overnight plus 2 hours on low or 5-6 hours on high

1. Put beans and water in crockpot on low overnight or for the day:

   2 C. navy or small white beans   **8 C. water**

2. Remove beans from crockpot, draining them and reserving bean liquid. Place in the crockpot and cook on low 2 hours or high 1 hour:

2 C. cooked beans	**3 ribs celery, chopped**
2 C. chicken broth *(p. 62 or 145)*	**2 cloves garlic, minced**
3 C. bean liquid,	**1 green chili, finely chopped**
plus water, as needed	**(fresh or canned)**
¹/₂ C. *Liquid Aminos**	**¹/₂ tsp. dry mustard**
1 onion, chopped	**2 bay leaves**

3. Puree remaining beans with liquid in blender and add to soup with green beans, meat; cook just until green beans are done, about 15-20 minutes:

remaining cooked beans	**10 oz. (2 C.) French cut green beans**
1 C. liquid	**2 C. cooked chicken or turkey,**
(bean and/or water)	**optional** *(p. 145)*

*An all-purpose soy seasoning available at health food stores.

VEGETARIAN ALTERNATIVE: Omit broth. Add **2 C. water** plus **1-2 tbsp. *Sue's Kitchen Magic*** to taste.

111

1 Turkey Burger, *using 90% fat-free ground turkey (approx. $1.35)*
Exchanges: 3 meat, 1.5 fat, 3.75 bread, 1 vegetable
529 calories
36 grams protein (27%)
22 grams fat (37%), 66 mg. cholesterol
48 grams carbohydrate (36%), 7.5 grams dietary fiber
625 mg. sodium

MENU

**569 Calories
34% Fat
$1.55***

TURKEY BURGERS (p. 113)

RELISH PLATE:

CARROT AND CELERY STICKS

CUCUMBER SLICES

COOKED CHILLED BROCCOLI (FLOWERS) (p. 156)

CAULIFLOWERETS

*For size servings on which data is based, see p. 12. To adjust fat level of menus, see p. 193.

4 Burgers

Very filling! Turkey burgers will not hold together as well as ground beef, so handle gently. The oat bran helps keep them together and adds valuable cholesterol-controlling fiber.

1. Mix together thoroughly and shape into 4 patties:

    1 lb. *Seasoned Ground Turkey* *(p. 149)*   **$^1/_2$ - $^3/_4$ C. oat bran**

2. Broil as for ground beef patties but not quite as long, or bake 10-15 minutes at 350°. These may also be fried but will not be as moist. No fat is needed in fry pan.

3. Serve with:

    4 whole grain hamburger buns *(p. 74)*   **sliced onions**
    Thousand Island Dressing *(p. 161)*   **alfalfa sprouts, optional**
        (2 tbsp. per serving)   **leafy lettuce**
    fresh tomato slices

VARIATION: In place of *Thousand Island Dressing* serve with **mayonnaise, ketchup, mustard, pickle relish** *(p. 94)*.

VEGETARIAN ALTERNATIVE: This actually happened! For a picnic we took all the burger fixin's but forgot to take the ground turkey patties! They tasted unexpectedly delicious with the addition of a **few slices of avocado. Tofu burger patties** are also available in some health food stores.

RAGOUT

1 serving of 4, using 90% fat-free ground turkey, unpeeled potatoes, salt and pepper excluded (approx. $1.05)

    Exchanges: 2.75 meat, 1.5 bread, 2.75 vegetable
    336 calories
    28 grams protein (32%)
    8.5 grams fat (22%), 66 mg. cholesterol
    40 grams carbohydrate (46%), 11.5 grams dietary fiber
    143 mg. sodium

MENU

778 Calories
18% Fat
$1.85*

RAGOUT (p. 115)
WITH 2 TBSP. KETCHUP

FROZEN CORN

BUTTERMILK DROP BISCUITS (p. 180)
WITH JAM

APPLE AND PINEAPPLE WEDGES (p. 92)

*For size servings on which data is based, see p. 12. To adjust fat level of menus, see p. 193.

Serves 4-6

Ra-goo, a childhood favorite, was made with ground beef and bacon. Our variation with ground turkey minus the bacon has continued to be a favorite family meal. Especially good with ketchup and frozen corn. I prefer this short-cooking method, but some enjoy using the crockpot.

1. In a wok or pan that has a tight-fitting lid and will hold all the ingredients, brown seasoned turkey:

   1 lb. *Seasoned Ground Turkey* *(p. 149)*

2. Layer over ground turkey:

   1 large onion, sliced   **4 medium potatoes, thinly sliced,**
   6 medium carrots, thinly sliced   **peeled or unpeeled**
   $^1\!/_2$ -1 C. water

3. Season with **salt and pepper, to taste**; cover tightly. Simmer until vegetables are tender, about 30 minutes. Check occasionally, stirring up from the bottom to prevent sticking. Add more water, if needed, but not too much.

CROCKPOT VARIATION: Brown the seasoned turkey and place with remaining ingredients in crockpot. **Add 1$^1\!/_2$ C. water**. Stir once. Cook on low 5-6 hours or high 2$^1\!/_2$ -3 hours.

VEGETARIAN ALTERNATIVE: Omit ground turkey. Add **1 C. chopped celery, 1 C. frozen peas** (add last 5 minutes of cooking). Top with **1 C. grated cheese.**

TUNA BUNSTEADS

½ bun with filling *(approx. $.60)*
  Exchanges: 1.5 meat, 1 fat, 1.5 bread, 0.5 vegetable
  262 calories
  18.5 grams protein (28%)
  11 grams fat (38%), 64 mg. cholesterol
  22 grams carbohydrate (34%), 3 grams dietary fiber
  520 mg. sodium

MENU

762 Calories
33% Fat
$1.80*

2 TUNA BUNSTEADS *(p. 117)*

ARRANGED TOMATO/CUCUMBER SALAD *(p. 158)*
WITH HERB VINEGAR

CARROT STICKS

2 CHOCO-CAROB NO-BAKE COOKIES *(p. 192)*

*For size servings on which data is based, see p. 12. To adjust fat level of menus, see p. 193. The cookies in this menu do not raise the percentage of fat.

4-6 Bunsteads

Kid-pleasing open-faced hot sandwiches! If whole grain hot dog buns are not available, use whole grain hamburger buns or bread.

1. Cut hot dog buns open and lay face up on cookie sheet. Toast lightly at 350° for 5-10 minutes; remove from oven:

   2-3 whole grain hot dog buns *(p. 74)*

2. In a mixing bowl combine remaining ingredients and spread evenly over lightly toasted bun halves on cookie sheet:

   **6.5 oz. can tuna, water-pack,
   well drained**
   ¹/₂ C. grated cheddar cheese
   2 tbsp. mayonnaise *(p. 94)*
   2 tbsp. nonfat yogurt
   1 tbsp. sweet pickle relish *(p. 94)*

   1 hard-cooked egg, chopped
   **¹/₄ C. sliced ripe olives, drained
   (half of 2¹/₄ oz. can)**
   1 tbsp. chopped green pepper
   1 tbsp. chopped onion

3. Return to oven to bake at 250° about 30 minutes until filling is hot and cheese melted.

117

1 serving of 8, *excluding rice (approx. $2.25)*
Exchanges: 5.25 meat, 0.75 milk, 1.5 fat, 2 bread, 0.5 fruit, 0.25 vegetable
625 calories
53 grams protein (34%)
29.5 grams fat (43%), 133 mg. cholesterol
37 grams carbohydrate (23%), 4 grams dietary fiber
1,083 mg. sodium (due to using canned soups!)

MENU

966 Calories
28% Fat
$3.00*

JAVANESE DINNER (p. 119)

BROWN RICE (p. 148)

FANTASTIC BROCCOLI (p. 156)

COUNTRY GELATIN SALAD (p. 159)

For size servings on which data is based, see p. 12. To adjust fat level of menus, see p. 193.

A frequently served company meal, this is a real crowd pleaser! It is our only recipe calling for canned cream soup. Preparation is fast if chicken is cooked and shredded in advance.

1. Make a double recipe of *Brown Rice*, p. 148.

2. Blend broth with soups in saucepan over low heat until very hot, but not boiling, stirring to prevent sticking, as needed; gently fold in chicken (over-stirring will make the chicken unpleasantly stringy):

   1¼ C. chicken broth* *(p. 62 or 145)*   **4 C. cooked chicken** *(p. 145)*
   10 oz. can cream of chicken soup*   **(about 2½ lbs. boneless breast)**
   10 oz. can cream of celery soup*

3. Prepare topping ingredients; place in separate serving dishes or on a lazy Susan (that's not me!):

   9.5 oz. can chow mein noodles*   **½ C. almonds (slivered, sliced,**
   2 chopped green onions   **or chopped)**
   2 large ribs celery, chopped small   **¼ C. shredded coconut***
   20 oz. can pineapple chunks, drained* **2 C. finely grated cheddar cheese**

4. **To Serve:** Pour sauce over rice, add toppings as desired—Yum!

I use unsalted broth, reduced salt soups, **China Boy brand noodles, unsweetened pineapple and coconut. I cut pineapple chunks in half for smaller pieces.*

VEGETARIAN ALTERNATIVE: Omit broth, chicken, chicken soup. Use **Campbell's Healthy Request** cream of mushroom soup, 4 C. sliced fresh mushrooms, 1¼ C. water plus 1¼ tsp. **Sue's Kitchen Magic**, to taste *(p. 52)*.

TACO CHIP OLÉ

1 serving of 6, *using 90% fat-free ground turkey, excluding salsa and yogurt/sour cream (approx. $1.25)*

> *Exchanges: 3.5 meat, .25 fat, 2.75 bread, 1.75 vegetable*
> *446 calories*
> *26 grams protein (23%)*
> *23 grams fat (45%), 68 mg. cholesterol*
> *37 grams carbohydrate (32%), 8 grams dietary fiber*
> *522 mg. sodium*

MENU

762 Calories
34% Fat
$2.10*

TACO CHIP OLÉ (p. 121)
WITH LIGHT SOUR CREAM/NONFAT YOGURT
(¹/4 C. EACH)

SALSA

BANANA CHUNKS, ORANGE SLICES,
AND PINEAPPLE WEDGES (p. 92)

1 C. APPLE JUICE

For size servings on which data is based, see p. 12. To adjust fat level of menus, see p. 193.

TACO CHIP OLÉ

Serves 4-6

A crowd-pleasing certainty! Sauce freezes well.

1. Season and brown turkey, adding onion when about half done:

   1 lb. *Seasoned Ground Turkey* *(p. 149)*   **¹/₂ C. chopped onion**

2. Add to turkey and onion, bring to boil, lower heat and simmer 15 minutes to blend flavors, stirring occasionally:

   12 oz. can tomato sauce,   **¹/₁₆ tsp. cumin powder**
   ** no salt added** *(p. 94)*   **dash oregano**
   ³/₄ tsp. chili powder   **³/₈ tsp. salt, to taste**
   ¹/₄ tsp. garlic powder   **(add after it simmers 15 minutes)**

3. Meanwhile, assemble in separate serving dishes for the table:

   1¹/₄ C. grated cheddar cheese   **2¹/₄ oz. can sliced ripe olives**
   2 C. shredded leafy lettuce   **8 oz. corn chips**
   2 C. shredded iceberg lettuce   **¹/₂ - ³/₄ cup yogurt/sour cream blend,***
   2 medium tomatoes, chopped small   **optional**
   salsa

4. **To Serve:** Pile sauce over chips and add toppings, as desired.

*Blend equal portions of fat-free or light sour cream and nonfat or lowfat yogurt.

VEGETARIAN ALTERNATIVE: Omit turkey. Add sautéed: **1 chopped green pepper, 1 C. sliced fresh mushrooms, ¹/₂ C. each chopped celery and carrot**. Use **chopped avocado** in place of grated cheese, if desired.

121

# LEMON BAKED FISH

1 serving of 3, using red snapper (approx. $1.80)
    Exchanges: 3.25 meat, 0.5 vegetable
    211 calories
    41.5 grams protein (82%)
    2.5 grams fat (10%), 76 mg. cholesterol
    4 grams carbohydrate (8%), 1 gram dietary fiber
    124 mg. sodium

MENU

563 Calories
11% Fat
$2.85*

LEMON BAKED FISH *(p. 123)*
WITH 2 TBSP. TARTAR SAUCE *(p. 123)*
AND LEMON WEDGE

³/₄ C. MEXICAN RICE *(p. 47)*

STEAMED ZUCCHINI
WITH GREEN PEPPER STRIPS AND BASIL

FRUIT SHRUB *(p. 184)*
OR SLICED ORANGES

For size servings on which data is based, see p. 12. To adjust fat level of menus, see p. 193.

LEMON BAKED FISH

4 Servings

One of our two most often used fish recipes. Simple and tasty! Excellent for any lean fish such as halibut, cod, fillet of sole, red snapper. Serve with tartar sauce, if desired.

1. Pour a little of the lemon juice in baking pan; add fish in single layer; pour over remaining lemon juice, sprinkle with seasoning and onion:

   1 lb. fish fillet or steak   **1¼ tsp. *Sue's Fish Herb Seasoning****
   juice of 1 lemon (¼ C.)   **½ small onion, thinly sliced, optional**

2. Bake at 350° for 20-30 minutes, basting 2 or 3 times until fish is opaque and flakes easily.

**Sue's Fish Herb Seasoning:* Blend 1 tbsp. each of the following; store in tightly covered container in cupboard for ready use. Enough for 12 lbs. fish:

onion powder	**dried parsley flakes**	**paprika**
dill weed	**thyme leaves, crushed**	**garlic powder**

TARTAR SAUCE

Scant ½ Cup

Try this reduced fat version! Thoroughly whisk together:

⅓ C. nonfat yogurt   **⅛ tsp. garlic powder**
1 tbsp. mayonnaise *(p. 94)*   **⅛ tsp. dill weed**
1 tbsp. sweet pickle relish *(p. 94)*   **½ tsp. mustard, to taste** *(p. 94)*
1½ tsp. lemon juice

1 frank and bun, without condiments (approx. $.70)
   Exchanges: 2 meat, 3 bread
   335 calories
   15 grams protein (18%)
   14 grams fat (38%), 45 mg. cholesterol
   37 grams carbohydrate (44%), 4 grams dietary fiber
   1,051 mg. sodium (those wieners!)

MENU

618 Calories
31% Fat
$1.35*

HEALTHIER HOT DOG (p. 125)
**WITH 2 TBSP. KETCHUP, 1 TSP. MUSTARD,
2 TBSP. SWEET PICKLE RELISH**

1 OZ. CORN CHIPS (p. 177)

CARROT AND CELERY STICKS

APPLE

*For size servings on which data is based, see p. 12. To adjust fat level of menus, see p. 193.

Not aimed at nutritional utopia, just realistic improvement!

Assemble:
    whole wheat hot dog buns, heated *(p. 74)*
    chicken franks *(p. 82)*, **lightly broiled**
    ketchup *(p. 94)*
    mustard *(p. 94)*
    sweet pickle relish *(p. 94)*
    leafy lettuce, optional

VEGETARIAN ALTERNATIVE: Use **meatless franks**. I recommend *Health Valley* brand made with tofu. They contain wheat and they're not bad tasting!

1 serving of 4, relish, yogurt/sour cream, salsa not included (approx. $1.70)

   Exchanges: 6.25 meat, 4.5 bread

   684 calories

   37 grams protein (21%)

   38.5 grams fat (49%), 120 mg. cholesterol

   54.5 grams carbohydrate (30%), 12 grams dietary fiber

   2,272 mg. sodium (Blame it on the dog and the chili! See our meal average, p. xiii, for consolation.)

MENU

**740 Calories
45% Fat
$2.05***

CHILI DOG (p. 127)
WITH ½ C. SHREDDED LETTUCE AND ⅓ DICED TOMATO

RELISH PLATE:

CARROT STICKS

RADISHES

JICAMA STICKS

BELL PEPPER STRIPS

For size servings on which data is based, see p. 12. To adjust fat level of menus, see p. 193.

Serves 4

A very filling "I-hate-to-cook" meal!

1. **Prepare:**

    4 whole grain hot dog buns *(p. 74)*, **split open, lightly toasted**
    8 chicken franks *(p. 82)*, **lightly broiled**
    15 oz. *Health Valley Chili*,* **heated (mild or spicy vegetarian)**
    1 C. grated cheddar cheese
    sweet pickle relish *(p. 94)*
    chopped tomatoes
    shredded lettuce
    salsa, optional
    yogurt/sour cream blend,** optional

2. **To Serve:** Cut franks lengthwise and arrange on toasted buns; top with chili and cheese; garnish with tomatoes and lettuce. Top with salsa and yogurt/sour cream blend, if desired.

   * ***Health Valley*** *products are available in most health food stores and some supermarkets.*

** *For yogurt/sour cream, blend equal portions of fat-free or light sour cream with nonfat or lowfat yogurt.*

VEGETARIAN ALTERNATIVE: Use **meatless franks**. (*Health Valley* brand are made with tofu and contain wheat.)

127

POTATO TOSTADAS

1 tostada, using 90% fat-free ground turkey (approx. $.50)
 Exchanges: 1.25 meat, 0.25 milk, 1.5 bread, 1 fat, 0.25 vegetable
 254 calories
 15 grams protein (23%)
 9 grams fat (32%), 24 mg. cholesterol
 29 grams carbohydrate (45%), 4 grams dietary fiber
 227 mg. sodium

MENU

765 Calories
27% Fat
$1.80*

2 POTATO TOSTADAS (p. 129)

TOSSED SALAD (p. 158)
WITH HERB VINEGAR

YOGURT PIE (p. 188)

*For size servings on which data is based, see p. 12. To adjust fat level of menus, see p. 193.

6 Tostadas

This fun meal is a great way to use leftover cooked or baked potatoes. If potatoes are cooked and the turkey seasoned and browned in advance, it is quick to assemble.

1. **To crisp tortillas:** Rub each tortilla on both sides with oil using a piece of wax paper; set directly on oven rack and bake at 350° for 10 minutes or to desired crispness:

   6 stoneground corn tortillas *(p. 177)*   **¹/₂ tsp. canola oil *(each tortilla)***

2. Season and brown turkey:

1 lb. ground turkey *(p. 42)*	**¹/₂ tsp. nutmeg**
¹/₈ tsp. cayenne pepper	**¹/₂ tsp. thyme**
1 tsp. *Sue's Kitchen Magic* *(p. 52),*	**¹/₂ tsp. sage**
optional	**¹/₂ tsp. salt**

3. Steam onion until tender, adding potatoes to heat them through:

   ¹/₃ C. chopped onion   **2 cooked potatoes, peeled, chopped**

4. Mash avocado with juice and salt; in separate bowl blend sour cream with the milk:

1 medium avocado	**¹/₂ C. fat-free sour cream** *(p. 72)*
2 tsp. lemon juice	**2 tbsp. lowfat milk**
¹/₈ tsp. salt, to taste	

5. **To Serve:** Spread over tortillas in order: mashed avocado, turkey, potato/onion, sour cream/milk. Add **salsa**, if desired.

6 oz. potato, *peeled, without additions (approx. $.30)*
  Exchanges: 3 bread
  198 calories
  3 grams protein (6%)
  no fat!
  46 grams carbohydrate (91%), 7 grams dietary fiber
  17 mg. sodium

MENU

628 Calories
20% Fat
$1.30*

6 OZ. BAKED YAM *(p. 131)*
WITH ½ C. CRUSHED PINEAPPLE
AND 1 TBSP. BUTTER SPREAD *(p. 171)*

CABBAGE-CARROT SALAD *(p. 158)*
WITH SWEET LITE DRESSING *(p. 160)*

FROZEN OR FRESH GREEN BEANS

HOT ROLLS *(p. 164)*
WITH JAM

*For size servings on which data is based, see p. 12. To adjust fat level of menus, see p. 193.

Yes! A baked yam* or sweet potato can be the main item for dinner, even for a "meat-eater"! Moisten with orange juice or enjoy with crushed pineapple to reduce the need for too much butter. Try eating the skins for an unexpected taste surprise.

1. Pierce scrubbed whole potatoes with a fork in several places to allow steam to escape.

2. Place potatoes directly on oven rack in center of oven.

3. Place a piece of foil on bottom of oven to catch possible spills from baking potatoes.

4. Bake at 400° uncovered** until tender when pierced with a fork, about 1 hour.

* *Yams available in USA are not true yams, but a variety of sweet potatoes. They are much higher in vitamin A than true yams.*

** *If baking something else at the same time that requires 350°, the potatoes can be baked at this temperature. Just add an extra 30 minutes or so to the baking time.*

1 serving, *using smaller amounts of ingredients in recipe (approx. $1.55)*
Exchanges: 1.5 meat, 3.25 bread, 4 fat, 0.75 vegetable
511 calories
19 grams protein (14%)
25.5 grams fat (44%), 7 mg. cholesterol
56 grams carbohydrate (42%), 10.5 grams dietary fiber
600 mg. sodium

MENU

613 Calories
36% Fat
$1.60*

NATURALLY NACHOS *(p. 133)*

OR

POOR MAN'S SANDWICH *(p. 133)*

CARROT AND CELERY STICKS

APPLE

For size servings on which data is based, see p. 12. To adjust fat level of menus, see p. 193.

❧ NATURALLY NACHOS ❧

Serves 1

Another one of my chief "I-hate-to-cook" meals, ready in less than 15 minutes. Use a 16 oz. can **Rosarita Vegetarian Refried Beans**.

1. Put the chips on a plate, top with remaining ingredients in order given and place uncovered in oven at 350° until cheese melts, 5-10 minutes:

    2-3 oz. (1½ -2½ C.) corn chips *(p. 177)*
    ½ -1 C. vegetarian refried beans, heated
    ¼ -⅓ C. grated cheddar cheese

2. Top with:

    1 chopped green onion
    ½ small or medium tomato, diced

3. For optional extras add **salsa, yogurt/sour cream, avocado, onion, chilies.**

❧ POOR MAN'S SANDWICH ❧

Another way to get a meal out of a can of **Rosarita Vegetarian Refried Beans**.

Put these ingredients and any *Naturally Nacho* extras (steps 2 and 3 above) between **2 halves whole grain bun** or **French roll**:

mayonnaise *(p. 94)*	**chopped cucumber, optional**
vegetarian refried beans	**thinly sliced celery, optional**
garlic and onion powder, to taste	**leaf lettuce, optional**

8 oz. baked potato, *salt and pepper to taste, avocado not included (approx. $1.20)*
    Exchanges: 1 meat, 4.5 bread, 3.7 fat, 2 vegetable
    590 calories
    18 grams protein (12%)
    23 grams fat (34%), 23 mg. cholesterol
    84 grams carbohydrate (55%), 19 grams dietary fiber
    139 mg. sodium

MENU

BAKED POTATO GOURMET *(p. 135)*

1 C. TOMATO JUICE

LITE CHOCOLATE PUDDING *(p. 186)*

776 Calories
27% Fat
$1.75*

*For size servings on which data is based, see p. 12. To adjust fat level of menus, see p. 193.

An elegantly served baked potato with lots of color and taste! Have all the ingredients ready to pre-pare the potato as soon as it is baked and serve immediately.

1. Bake **good sized potato, about 8 oz.** *(p. 137)*.

2. Set potato in center of lettuce in wide shallow soup bowl or salad plate and top with remaining ingredients in order given:

   > **bed of leafy lettuce (butterhead is especially nice)**
   > **hot baked potato (cut and squeeze open)**
   > **1 tbsp.** *Butter Spread* *(p. 171)* **or butter**
   > **1/2 C. frozen or fresh hot corn**
   > **1/4 C. grated cheddar cheese**

3. Garnish with:

   > **1/2 tomato, cut in wedges**
   > **sautéed vegetables:**
   > > **1/2 medium zucchini, sliced**
   > > **1/2 C. mushroom slices**
   > > **1/4 green pepper, cut in strips**
   >
   > **Worcestershire sauce** *(p. 94)***, to taste**
   > **avocado slices, optional**

8 oz. baked potato, *with skin (approx. $.30)*
Exchanges: 2.5 bread
165 calories
4.5 grams protein (11%)
no fat!
37.5 grams carbohydrate (88%), 9.5 grams dietary fiber (5 grams without the skin)
5 mg. sodium

MENU

593 Calories
18% Fat
$2.05*

BAKED POTATO BAR *(p. 137)*

¾ C. CHICKEN CURRY *(p. 17)*

FROZEN OR FRESH GREEN PEAS

TOSSED SALAD *(p. 158)*
WITH SWEET ORANGE DRESSING *(p. 160)*

*For size servings on which data is based, see p. 12. To adjust fat level of menus, see p. 193.

*Make a party of this meal with several topping choices or keep it simple with a saucy leftover for the topping. If small amounts of saucy dishes are left over, haven't been previously frozen, and are freezable, freeze them until you have enough for a **Baked Potato Bar** meal.*

Bake: 400° for 1 hour or 350° for about 1½ hours, uncovered

1. For each serving scrub, oil lightly, if desired, and bake at 400° directly on oven rack (or at 350° if baking something else at that temperature):

   8 oz. potato

2. Slit baked potatoes lengthwise, but not quite through. Squeeze it crosswise to fluff and soften.

3. Add toppings, as desired; allow ½ -¾ C. sauce topping per serving:

   Chicken Curry (p. 17)   *Chili Gourmet* (p. 87)
   Turkey-Mushroom Sauce (p. 59)   *Javanese Dinner chicken sauce* (p. 119)
   Spaghetti-Joe Sauce (p. 79)   *Taco Chip Olé sauce* (p. 121)

4. **Other Options:**

   grated ceddar cheese   **minced parsley or chives**
   chopped onion or green onion **sunflower seeds, unsalted**
   chopped green pepper   **Parmesan cheese**
   celery, sliced thinly on diagonal **chopped nuts**

1 pizza with large pita bread, *choice of vegetable topping not included (approx. $.80)*
  Exchanges: 1.75 meat, 3 bread, 0.5 fat, 1.25 vegetable
  358 calories
  20 grams protein (21%)
  11.5 grams fat (28%), 19 mg. cholesterol
  45 grams carbohydrate (50%), 5.5 grams dietary fiber
  811 mg. sodium

MENU

649 Calories
30% Fat
$1.75*

IN-A-MINUTE PIZZA *(p. 139)*

TOSSED SALAD *(p. 158)*
WITH LEMON-OLIVE OIL DRESSING *(p. 161)*

FRUIT SHRUB *(p. 184)*
OR ORANGE AMBROSIA *(p. 182)*

For size servings on which data is based, see p. 12. To adjust fat level of menus, see p. 193.

1 Individual Pizza

Whole grain pita breads make the perfect crust for speed pizzas! English muffin halves make good runner-ups.

Oven: 350° until cheese melts, uncovered

1. Place pita bread bottom-side up on cookie sheet and spread with remaining ingredients:

> **1 large whole grain pita bread** *(p. 164)*
> **¼ C. spaghetti or pasta sauce** *(p. 94)*
>   **or tomato sauce with Italian seasoning**
> **1 tbsp. Parmesan cheese**
> **¼ C. mozzarella cheese**
> **2 tbsp. sliced ripe olives**

2. Add optional desired vegetables, raw or lightly sauteed in olive oil:

> **chopped onion or green onion**
> **chopped bell pepper**
> **sliced mushrooms**
> **chopped artichoke hearts, canned water-pack**

GOLDEN WAFFLES

1-1¹/₂ 7" waffle, oil included *(approx. $.40)*
  Exchanges: 0.25 meat, 0.5 milk, 3.25 bread, 1.5 fat
  369 calories
  11 grams protein (12%)
  12 grams fat (29%), 74 mg. cholesterol
  56 grams carbohydrate (59%), 8 grams dietary fiber
  728 mg. sodium

MENU

770 Calories
22% Fat
$1.55*

1¹/₂-2¹/₄ 7" GOLDEN WAFFLES *(p. 141)*

ALICE'S FRUIT SOUP *(p. 142)*
WITH ¹/₃ BANANA, SLICED
(A YUMMY WAFFLE TOPPING!)

¹/₄ C. LOWFAT VANILLA YOGURT

*For size servings on which data is based, see p. 12. To adjust fat level of menus, see p. 193.

GOLDEN WAFFLES ≈≈≈

7-9 7" Waffles ~ Serves 5-6

With this blender recipe these waffles can be ready to bake in 5 minutes—a deliciously quick way to add whole grains to the diet without owning a flour mill. This recipe and its possible grain variations make it worth having a good blender and a waffle iron! This is my first-choice "I-hate-to-cook" evening meal.

1. Put in the blender and blend on high speed for 3 minutes:

> **2¼ C. buttermilk (or yogurt thinned to buttermilk consistency)**
> **2 medium eggs (may be entirely omitted, if desired)**
> **3 tbsp. olive or canola oil** (p. 171)**, optional (adds the crispness)**
> **1½ tsp. vanilla**
> **⅔ C. whole dry corn (not cornmeal, not flour)***
> **⅔ C. whole wheat pastry grain (not flour)***

2. Just before baking blend in briefly (stir in if blender won't take hold):

> **1 tbsp. baking powder** (p. 163)
> **¾ tsp. baking soda**
> **1½ tsp. salt**

3. Bake about 1½-2 minutes in hot waffle iron, lightly sprayed with non-stick spray, if needed. Do not overbake.

*Each grain is equivalent to 1½ C. flour. If using all flour (a total of 3 C.), blend just briefly to mix in. Almost any grain equivalent to 3 C. flour can be used successfully in place of corn and wheat, if desired. To use cornmeal in place of corn, add it after the 3-minute blend.

141

ALICE'S FRUIT SOUP

11 Cups (without bananas)

*A 5-minute recipe! Enjoy as a different type of dessert or a fantastic waffle topping! Leftover soup keeps well for several days without bananas. Try the delicious **Fruit Smoothie*** suggested below with the leftovers. Mm-mm good! Vary the fruits, as desired.*

1. Place *unsweetened* frozen fruit in a large bowl:

    12 oz. frozen raspberries (key ingredient)
    16 oz. frozen whole strawberries
    12 oz. frozen blueberries, boysenberries, or blackberries

2. Add, all *unsweetened, undrained*:

    20 oz. can pineapple chunks   **16 oz. pear halves (cut up halves)**
    16 oz. can peach slices (cut up slices)

3. Stir well to combine and distribute juices. Let stand about 2 hours at room temperature or in refrigerator overnight to become juicy and thawed.

4. **Optional:** Add just before serving, amount desired:

    sliced bananas (add only to portion to be immediately served)

1 C. (approx. $.70), Exchanges: 2 fruit; 118 calories, 30 grams carbohydrate (93%), 4.5 grams dietary fiber, 9 mg. sodium

Fruit Smoothie: Place in blender and blend on high speed until smooth: peeled chunks of 2 bananas, 1 peeled cut-up orange, about 1 C. **Alice's Fruit Soup, 3 ice cubes, ¹/₂ C. water. For extra sweetness, if desired, add 6 chopped dates and/or ¹/₄ C. unsweetened frozen juice concentrate, any blend. Makes 2 sumptuous servings.*

Potpourri

All the extras you need to complete
your main dish recipes and dinner menus successfully:
from cooking and freezing chicken and broth to using
quick-baking mixes and menu planning!

Freezing Chicken and Broth

TO FREEZE COOKED CHICKEN: Divide cooled cooked chicken into portion sizes desired. Wrap as tightly as possible to exclude air with plastic wrap, then wrap snuggly in aluminum foil. Label with date and amount. Use frozen chicken packed dry in this way within one month. Cooked chicken packed in gravy or sauce will keep frozen for up to six months (use plastic containers for packing in a sauce or gravy). Remove the wraps before heating in any way.

TO FREEZE BROTH: When broth is cooled and fat skimmed off the top, pour desired portions into plastic containers leaving at least 1/2" head space. Cover tightly and freeze. When frozen, snap the frozen block from the container by running hot water over the entire surface until it comes out easily. Wrap securely in plastic wrap, then foil. (Tip: Stick the freezer label on the foil before you wrap it around the frozen broth. Otherwise, the cold penetrating the foil from the broth will keep the label from sticking.) Use the broth within 6 months.

Quick Method: *For quick "on-the-spot" cooking, cut the chicken for chunks and cook in gently boiling water about 20 minutes or until tender. For shredded chicken, cook pieces whole and shred after cooking. The cooking water can be used for broth, though not as flavorful as the recipe below.*

Slow-Cooking Method: *This is a great way to prepare a larger quantity of chicken in advance while producing tasty broth that may be used for several dishes. Use freshly cooked chicken for dishes to be frozen. Frozen chicken can be used in dishes that won't be frozen (chicken should not be refrozen). Use either fresh or frozen broth for any dish.*

Amount: About 3-4 Quarts Broth, 5-6 Cups Chicken

1. Place together in large pot or crockpot:

   4-5 lbs. chicken, whole or parts   **few sprigs fresh parsley**
   4 qts. water   **1 bay leaf**
   small onion, chopped   **$\frac{1}{2}$ tsp. marjoram leaves**
   handful celery leaves, chopped   **$\frac{1}{4}$ tsp. sweet basil leaves**
   couple of carrots, chopped   **2 tsp. salt, optional**

2. **Crockpot:** Low 8-10 hours, or high $3\frac{1}{2}$ -$4\frac{1}{2}$ hours. **Large Pot:** Bring slowly to boil, cover and lower heat; simmer 2-3 hours; add more water, if needed, to keep meat or bones covered.

3. Place colander in large bowl; drain. Cool 30 minutes. Discard vegetables, skin, bone. Refrigerate broth to let fat rise to top. Skim off before using.

4. To freeze broth and chicken, see p. 144.

SHOPPER'S GUIDE TO...
LEGUMES AND GRAINS, NUTS AND SEEDS

LEGUMES (DRY BEANS): Most common kinds are readily available in supermarkets, but are seldom grown organically. Organically grown legumes as well as nonorganically grown are available in health food stores and through mail order sources.*

GRAINS: Brown rice, rolled oats, and whole wheat bread flour are the extent of offerings in most supermarkets. All grains and whole grain flours are available in many health food stores from 2-lb. to 5-lb. packages or in open stock bins.* For freshness and top nutritive value I recommend purchasing grains over whole grain flours (see pp. 165 and 166).

NUTS AND SEEDS: Unsalted, unroasted walnuts, almonds, pecans can usually be found in supermarkets, seeds in health food stores. Most, except walnuts, are usually less costly purchased in 1-lb. or 2-lb. packages in health food stores.

*Mail order sources offer 5-lb., 25-lb., 50-lb., 100-lb. bags of all these items at a savings, organic or nonorganic. **Jaffe Bros.** in Valley Center, California, (619) 749-1133, ships UPS and accepts credit card phone orders. Request a catalog.

Next to effortless way to cook up beans before using in a recipe! Cook up and freeze a quantity to have on hand at a moment's notice. Home-cooked dry beans avoid the high sodium content of canned beans.

Amount: 2 Cups Dry Beans (about 1 lb.) = 4-5 Cups Cooked Beans

1. Sort and wash desired amount of beans (e.g., kidney, black, pinto, navy, lima).

2. Place in crockpot and cover with $2\frac{1}{2}$-3 times the amount of water unless recipe specifies otherwise (e.g., 5-6 C. water to 2 C. beans).

3. Cook on low overnight or about $9\frac{1}{2}$ hours until tender (the older the beans, the longer it will take to cook them). If desired, cook on high in about half the time.

4. Drain to use in your recipe, or freeze in desired portions.

Ways to help "de-gas" the beans:

- Add **a tsp. of garlic powder** to cooking water.
- Presoak beans before cooking, several hours or overnight; drain and add fresh water to cook.
- Add to soaking water **3 tbsp. fresh chopped green chilies or a tsp. fennel seed.**
- Sprout the beans before cooking about 2 days. This method is especially helpful for people who *really* have a problem.

3 Cups ~ Serves 4-6

Of the range-top methods I've tried, this has been most successful for a small amount. Larger quantities are liable to be more moist. A rice cooker is ideal (see below), especially for larger quantities. Cooked brown rice may be frozen. I use freezer bags. Steam to reheat.

1. Place together in a saucepan with a tight-fitting lid, bring to a boil, and boil uncovered for 5 minutes:

   2-2½ C. water   **½ -1 tsp. salt, to taste, optional**
   1 C. brown rice *(p. 40)*   **or 1-2 tsp.** ***Sue's Kitchen Magic*** *(p. 52)*

2. Cover tightly and lower heat to lowest setting. Simmer for 40-60 minutes (long grain requires longer than short grain).

To test for doneness: *Do not uncover while cooking. At end of cooking time insert a spoon straight down through rice to bottom of pot, pressing a bit to one side. If no water remains, taste rice for tenderness. Do not stir. If not done, cover and cook 10 minutes longer, or as needed until done.*

RICE COOKER METHOD: Follow the rice cooker directions for operation, but ignore the rice-water measurements. The proportion of water to rice needs to be increased. Use **2 C. uncooked brown rice** to **4½ C. water**. Salt or season, as desired.

¾ C., long grain with 1 tsp. salt (approx. $.06)
   Exchanges: 2.25 bread; 167 calories, 3.5 grams protein (8%), 1 gram fat (5%), 36 grams carbohydrate (87%), 3.5 grams dietary fiber, 359 mg. sodium

1 lb. ~ 2-2¼ Cups Cooked

For pleasingly improved flavor, season ground turkey before browning! I also use this recipe for turkey burger patties. For ready availability, season and brown ground turkey for the freezer and wrap in desired size packages in the same way as cooked chicken (p. 144).

In a mixing bowl, mix together thoroughly with a fork and brown in fry pan without oil, breaking it up with spatula as it cooks; do not overcook (ground turkey cooks faster than ground beef):

> **1 lb. ground turkey** *(p. 42)*
> **¹/₈ tsp. nutmeg***
> **¹/₈ tsp. thyme or thyme leaves***
> **¹/₈ tsp. garlic powder***
> **¹/₈ tsp. sage***
> **2 tsp. soy sauce or Worcestershire sauce** *(p. 94)*
> **2 tbsp. ketchup or tomato sauce** *(p. 94)*

*In place of measuring these seasonings every time, use **¹/₂ tsp. Ground Turkey Seasoning Mix** *(p. 151).*

***1 lb.**, using 90% fat-free ground turkey, **Featherweight** no-salt ketchup, **Kikkoman Lite** soy sauce (approx. $2.99)*
  Exchanges: 11 meat; 688 calories, 92 grams protein (53%), 33 grams fat (43%), 262 mg. cholesterol, 6.5 grams carbohydrate (4%), 0.5 gram dietary fiber, 400 mg. sodium

Quick Brown Rice

- Available in most supermarkets.

- Cooks in 14-20 minutes.

- Nutritional value virtually the same as brown rice.

- Texture is slightly different.

- Freezing not recommended; the texture suffers.

- Follow the package directions for cooking. I don't recommend microwaving *(see p. 10)*.

- More expensive than brown rice.

Brown Rice Nutritional Value: *Brown rice is worthy of your cultivated taste! As a rich source of vitamin B-complex, iron, and calcium, it contains 5 times the thiamine (B-1) and vitamin E, 3 times the dietary fiber, niacin (B-3), B-6, and magnesium, twice the iron and pantothenic acid, and 50% more zinc than white rice. And although it is not high in total amount of protein, it is one of the best grain sources for protein because it is high in lysine, the amino acid in which many grains are low.*

Seasons 48 lbs.

Measure dry seasonings once out of one container for ground turkey instead of 4 times out of 4 containers each time you do it!

1. Blend together thoroughly:

   2 tbsp. nutmeg
   2 tbsp. thyme or thyme leaves
   2 tbsp. garlic powder
   2 tbsp. sage

2. Store in tightly covered container in cupboard.

3. Write on the label: **Ground Turkey Seasoning, $^1/_2$ tsp. per lb.**

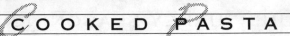

COOKED PASTA

2 oz. Raw = ¾ -1 Cup Cooked Pasta

For 1 lb. (16 oz.) pasta use 6-7 qts. water. I use this recipe for 8-12 oz. packages. For nutrient data and alternate cooking method, see p. 153. Cooked plain pasta freezes well. Steam to reheat.

1. Bring water to full rolling boil, add oil, salt; add pasta gradually to keep the water boiling:

4 qts. boiling water	**¼ tsp. salt**
1 tsp. olive oil	**8-12 oz. whole grain pasta** *(p. 20)*

2. Boil, following package directions for cooking time (usually 6-10 minutes).

For Freezer Dishes: *If cooking pasta to be frozen, cook it **al dente**, the Italian method of cooking until there is no starchy taste but a slight firmness to the bite. This will prevent over-cooking of the pasta when the frozen dish is reheated.*

3. Drain in colander. If cooked pasta sticks together,* use one of the following methods to separate it:

- **Toss with 1 tbsp. or less olive oil.**
- **Combine immediately with hot sauce or mixture it will be added to.**
- **Rinse in cold water (this will cause some nutrient loss).**

*Whole grain pastas do not stick together as readily as white pasta. Oil added to the cooking water also helps.

This method requires less attention and less fuel than the standard cooking method (p. 152).
For 1 lb. (16 oz.) pasta use 6-7 qts. water. I use this recipe for 8-12 oz. packages. 2 oz. raw pasta =
³/₄ C. cooked noodles or 1 C. cooked macaroni or spaghetti.

1. Bring water to full rolling boil, add oil, salt; add pasta gradually to keep the water boiling:

   4 qts. boiling water   **¹/₄ tsp. salt**
   1 tsp. olive oil   **8-12 oz. whole grain pasta** *(p.20)*

2. Cover tightly and remove from heat. Let stand for cooking time recommended on the pasta package, checking doneness after shorter recommended time. Let stand to the longer time, if needed; drain.

For Freezer Dishes: *If cooking pasta to be frozen, cook it **al dente**, the Italian method of cooking until there is no starchy taste but a slight firmness to the bite. This will prevent over-cooking of the pasta when the frozen dish is reheated.*

3. For ways to keep cooked pasta from sticking together, see p. 152. (This problem is minimized using whole grain pasta and oil in the cooking water.)

1 C. cooked pasta, *average of whole wheat, Kamut, spelt, salt and oil in water not included (approx. $.35)*
   Exchanges: 2.5 bread; 193 calories, 8.5 grams protein (18%), 2 grams fat (8%), 36 grams carbohydrate (74%), 6 grams dietary fiber, 4 mg. sodium

7 Popular Vegetables

DARK LEAFY GREENS—steamed spinach, chard, beet greens

BROCCOLI—*Fantastic Broccoli* (p. 156); fresh cooked, hot, or chilled

GREEN PEAS—frozen or fresh cooked

CORN—frozen or fresh cut or corn on the cob cooked

GREEN BEANS—frozen or fresh cooked

CARROTS—fresh cooked

CARROT/CELERY STICKS—raw

CHOOSE 1—cabbage, beets, cauliflower, asparagus, zucchini, broiled tomato slices, yellow squash

Lettuce Wash 'n Dry!

*F*or fresh salads in 5 minutes, this really works!

1. Fill sink with cool water.

2. Separate lettuce leaves and swish in water; repeat as necessary and drain in colander.

3. Put leaves in *lingerie bag* (that's right!).

4. Close bag and take it to the washing machine (right again!).

5. Put bag in clean washer and set on spin for 1 or 2 minutes.*

6. Put lettuce leaves in a plastic bag and refrigerate the cleanest, driest lettuce ever for instant salad making!

Or give the bag to your husband or one of the kids to swing over his head in the backyard!

❧❧ FANTASTIC BROCCOLI ❧❧

A no-fail method for bright crisp-tender broccoli every time! Chilled broccoli cooked this way keeps well in refrigerator 2-3 days. Broccoli has more than its share of valuable nutrients—a high source of vitamins A and C, with good amounts of calcium, potassium, and iron.

1. Purchase **1 lb. fresh broccoli for 3-4 servings.**

2. Wash and cut as desired. To peel tough outer layer of stalk, pull off with a paring knife.

3. Bring **enough water to cover broccoli** to a full boil.

4. Add broccoli to boiling water, returning to boil over high heat.

5. **Boil 40-60 seconds.** That's all!

6. Drain immediately in colander.

VARIATIONS:
- Sprinkle with **lemon juice** just before serving (sooner will turn it sickly yellow).
- Add steamed **julienne carrots** or **cauliflowerets.**
- Served **chilled** in tossed salads or relish plate.

³/₄ C. serving (approx. $.15)
  Exchanges: 1.5 vegetable; 35 calories, 3.5 grams protein (33%), 6.5 grams carbohydrate (60%), 2.5 grams dietary fiber, 13 mg. sodium

8" or 9" Square Pan ~ Serves 9-12

Gelatin with real fruit juice and no refined sugar!

1. In small saucepan whisk gelatin into juice; let stand 5 minutes; heat to boiling, stirring constantly to dissolve gelatin; stir in honey:

   ¾ C. orange juice
   1½ packages unflavored gelatin (3 tsp. or 1 tbsp.)
   3 tbsp. honey

2. Combine in mixing bowl:

   8 oz. can crushed pineapple,   **1 orange, chopped**
   unsweetened, drained   **1 banana, sliced**
   6 oz. can pineapple juice,   **¼ C. chopped pecans**
   (¾ C.), unsweetened   **or sliced almonds, optional**

3. Blend in **hot juice mixture** and pour into 8" or 9" pan, salad bowl, or individual molds, as desired.

4. Refrigerate until set.

5. **To Serve:** Cut in squares and serve plain or on bed of leafy lettuce, garnish of parsley or mint leaves. Top with *Sweet Mayonnaise* or *Sweet Lite Dressing (p. 160)*, or a blend of yogurt and sour cream in equal portions.

***1 serving of 9**, excluding nuts (approx. $.15)*
   Exchanges: 1.25 fruit; 80 calories, 2 grams protein (8%), 20 grams carbohydrate (92%), 1 gram dietary fiber, 2 mg. sodium

7 Easy Salads

TOSSED: Include dark leafy greens, 4 or 5 fresh vegetables; serve with an herb vinegar, oil, *Lemon-Olive Oil* (p. 161) or *Sweet Orange Dressing* (p. 160).

CABBAGE: Shredded cabbage, chunk fresh or unsweetened canned pineapple, and/or grated carrot with *Sweet Mayonnaise* or *Sweet Lite Dressing* (p. 160).

ORANGE-LETTUCE-BANANA: Tossed dark leafy lettuce greens, sliced banana, chopped orange with *Sweet Mayonnaise* or *Sweet Lite Dressing* (p. 160).

CARROT-RAISIN: Grated carrot, raisins, optional pineapple, apple, celery with *Sweet Mayonnaise* or *Sweet Lite Dressing* (p. 160).

ARRANGED: On leafy greens: tomato/cucumber (or avocado) slices with herb vinegar or cottage cheese (with yogurt blended in is good), or sliced oranges/pineapple spears with *Sweet Mayonnaise* or *Sweet Lite Dressing* (p. 160).

GELATIN: *Pineapple Orange Gelatin* (p. 157) or *Country Gelatin Salad* (p. 159), serve over leafy lettuce, dollop sour cream or *Sweet Mayonnaise* (p. 160).

WALDORF: chopped celery, apple, walnuts with *Sweet Mayonnaise* or *Sweet Lite Dressing* (p. 160).

Serves 4-6

Delicious berry-red gelatin with real fruit juice and no refined sugar!

1. In small saucepan whisk gelatin into juice; let stand for 5 minutes to soften gelatin; bring to a boil, stirring constantly, to dissolve gelatin; blend in honey; remove from heat:

   1 C. red, real juice (such as *Dole Pure and Light Country Raspberry Juice*)
   1 package (2 tsp.) unflavored gelatin*
   ¼ C. honey

2. Blend juice mixture into remaining ingredients in salad bowl or mold and refrigerate until set:

   1 C. red, real juice
     (same as above)
   1 C. frozen raspberries
   2 medium bananas, peeled, sliced
     (may be added after partially set, if desired)

*Contrary to what other books and charts say, 1 package unflavored gelatin contains only 2 tsp., not 1 tbsp.

1 serving of 6 *(approx. $.50)*
   Exchanges: 2 fruit; 139 calories, 2 grams protein (5%), 36 grams carbohydrate (95%), 4 grams dietary fiber, 6 mg. sodium

SWEET MAYONNAISE

Modify the fat with part yogurt! Delicious dressing for cabbage, carrot, fruit, Waldorf salads.

Whisk together thoroughly:

¼ C. mayonnaise	**1½ tsp. crystalline fructose** *(p. 163)* **or honey**
¼ C. nonfat yogurt	**1½ tsp. lemon juice**

1 tbsp. (approx. $.06), Exchanges: 1.25 fat; 62 calories, 6 grams fat (88%), 44 mg. sodium

SWEET LITE DRESSING

Eliminate the fat with yogurt! A light and tasty alternative for cabbage, carrot, fruit, Waldorf salads.

Whisk together thoroughly:

¼ C. nonfat yogurt	**2 tsp. crystalline fructose** *(p. 163)* **or honey**
⅛ tsp. salt	**2 tsp. lemon juice**

1 tbsp. (approx. $.06), Exchanges: 0.25 milk; 15 calories, 1 gram protein (21%), 3 grams carbohydrate (78%), 75 mg. sodium

SWEET ORANGE DRESSING

Surprisingly refreshing, tasty, effortless, and s-o-o-o nonfat! Good on most salads.

Squeeze and pour over salad, tossing lightly:

juice of ½ orange (That's right! Just the juice of half an orange!)

~~LEMON-OLIVE OIL DRESSING~~

1 Cup

An incredible dressing with a little hot bite! The use of quality oils may be more important to heart health and cholesterol levels than the amount. Olive oil is a healthful monounsaturated fat. I prefer to use extra virgin olive oil.

Gradually whisk oil into remaining ingredients; refrigerate to chill:

1 tsp. grated lemon peel	**1 tsp. crystalline fructose** *(p. 163)*
¼ C. fresh lemon juice	**or sugar**
1 tsp. salt	**4-6 drops Tabasco sauce**
¼ tsp. pepper	**¾ C. olive oil**

1 tbsp. *(approx. $.10), Exchanges: 2 fat; 92 calories, 10 grams fat (98%)*

~~THOUSAND ISLAND DRESSING~~

2½ Cups

Use yogurt to stretch mayonnaise for a lower fat dressing or spread.

Whisk together thoroughly:

1¼ C. nonfat plain yogurt	**1½ tsp. crystalline fructose** *(p. 163)*
¾ C. mayonnaise *(p. 94)*	**¼ tsp. salt, optional**
¼ C. ketchup *(p. 94)*	**⅛ tsp. garlic powder**
1 tbsp. lemon juice	**1 tbsp. pickle relish** *(p. 94)*

2 tbsp. *(approx. $.10), Exchanges: 1.5 fat; 75 calories, 7 grams fat (87%)*

7 Delicious Breads

MUFFINS
(pp. 168, 170, 172, 174, 176)

CORNBREAD
(p. 178)

BISCUITS
(p. 180)

BAKED BROWN BREAD
(p. 169)

SOURDOUGH
purchased *(p. 164)*

HOT ROLLS
purchased *(p. 164)*

TORTILLAS
purchased *(p. 164)*

SHOPPER'S GUIDE TO...
BAKING MIX INGREDIENTS

WHOLE WHEAT PASTRY FLOUR: Comes from soft wheat with lower gluten content than whole wheat flour, making lighter baked goods prepared without yeast. Kamut or spelt may be successfully substituted in most baked goods and for thickening.

KAMUT OR SPELT FLOUR: These are terrific wheat flours that many persons allergic to wheat can actually tolerate. They have their own wonderful flavor and texture.

CRYSTALLINE FRUCTOSE: This sugar usually comes from corn and is equally as refined as white sugar, yet it causes less insulin release into the bloodstream. Since crystalline fructose is sweeter than sugar, it can usually be substituted in half the amount. More nutritious alternatives to experiment with include *Sucanat* (whole sugar cane) and *Fruitsource* (from rice and grapes).

LOW SODIUM BAKING POWDER: Contains no corn or aluminum; 1 tsp. contains 2 mg. sodium compared to 200 mg. in others. *Rumford* (available in supermarkets) is not low sodium and contains corn, but it has no aluminum.

SALT: An unrefined or "sun-evaporated only" sea salt is the best type to use.

SHOPPER'S GUIDE TO...
WHOLE GRAIN BREADS

•*Sandwich Loaf Breads* •*Pita Bread* •*Tortillas*
•*English Muffins* •*Rolls* •*Sourdough* •*Buns* •*French Rolls*

YOUR LOCAL HEALTH FOOD STORE IS THE PLACE TO FIND WHOLE GRAIN BREADS.

INGREDIENTS LABELS—WHAT TO LOOK FOR: 100% whole wheat flour (stone-ground is best), sprouted grains, other whole flours; vegetable oil or no oil; nuts, seeds; honey, raisin syrup, barley malt, or no sweetening; water, sea salt; yeast or no yeast

INGREDIENTS LABELS—WHAT TO AVOID*: wheat flour (means white), white enriched flour, bleached white flour, unbleached white flour (preferred over bleached, but all whole grain is better); hydrogenated or partially hydrogenated vegetable oils, shortening, margarine; white or brown sugar, corn sweetener, corn syrup, dextrose; monodiglycerides, dough conditioners, unpronounceable chemicals

*It is difficult to find any breads without some of these ingredients in supermarkets.

Using Quick Mixes

THE KEY TO NUTRITION IS FRESHNESS OF THE FLOUR!

Rancid flours are hazardous to health. Whole grain flour is generally safe from rancidity at room temperature for about 1 month, or 1 year in refrigerator or freezer. The nutritional value, however, declines much faster, beginning as soon as oxidation occurs when the flour is milled. Therefore:

- When purchasing, inquire when the flour was milled. Try to find flour milled within a day or two of purchase. Have someone grind it for you, if possible.

- Make the quick mix immediately and refrigerate or freeze it (preferred) in airtight bags.

- Make only what will be used in a month or two.

Baking powder and soda lose their rising power after months on the shelf. To test, whisk 1 tsp. into $1/3$ C. hot water. Vigorous fizz and bubbles indicates good activity. Baking powder shelf life is 6 months, baking soda, $1^1/2$ years.

For satisfying results in rising and texture, bring quick mix to room temperature before adding liquid ingredients. Once mixed, bake immediately in preheated oven.

For the Best Flour!

**THERE IS NOTHING LIKE FRESH MILLED FLOURS
FROM A VARIETY OF WHOLE GRAINS!**

- Lighter—tastier—variety.

- More nutrients retained.

- Grains are easier to find and store than fresh flours.

- Whole grains lower in cost than flours.

- Write to *Eating Better Cookbooks* for grain mill information (address on p. 210).

Makes 4 Dozen Muffins

Mix up a delicious variety of muffins (see pp. 168-74) with this home-prepared ready mix! See pp. 163 and 165 for information on using mixes and purchasing ingredients.

1. Blend together thoroughly by sifting or stirring through a large strainer to break up any lumps:

   8 C. whole wheat pastry flour*   **2 tsp. baking soda**
   2 C. crystalline fructose   **4 tsp. salt**
   2 tbsp. baking powder

2. Store in tightly covered container in refrigerator or freezer up to 1 month. If desired evenly divide mix into four 6¹/₂" x 5 ⁷/₈" freezer bags. Each will make 10-12 muffins.** In each bag place:

   2¹/₄ C. plus 1¹/₄ tsp.

   Timesaver Tip: *For quick reference write page numbers of muffin recipes on packages.*

3. Important to the rising: Bring mix to *room temperature* before using.

* *Kamut or spelt flour (p. 163) may be substituted. When using spelt, reduce the liquid called for in muffins by about ¹/₄ the amount.*

** *Aside from miniature or giant muffin pans, the average muffin pan sizes are ¹/₃ C. deep or ¹/₄ C. deep. Normally a recipe makes 10 of the larger size muffins or 12 of the smaller. I prefer using the larger ¹/₃ C. deep muffin pan, filling 10 C. with batter and the center 2 with water (seems to help the rise).*

10-12 Muffins

*Our favorite bran muffin recipe using **Quick Muffin Mix**, p. 167.*

Bake: 350° for 20 minutes

1. Preheat oven. Spray muffin cups with non-stick spray or line with muffin papers (10 C. for larger muffin pan, 12 for smaller).

2. In small mixing bowl blend thoroughly and let stand 5 minutes to soften bran:
   1 C. wheat bran*   **½ C. boiling hot water**

3. In large mixing bowl whisk together thoroughly:
   1 egg   **1 C. buttermilk**

4. Blend into liquid ingredients, just until mixed (Do not overmix!):
   1 bag (2¼ C. plus 1¼ tsp.) Quick Muffin Mix *(p. 167)***, room temperature softened bran mixture**

5. Fill muffin cups evenly with batter; fill any empty cups half full of water. Bake until done, about 20 minutes. Cool in pan 5 minutes before removing if not using muffin papers.

*Plain bran, not cereal; less expensive in health food store than supermarket.

VARIATIONS: Fold in ½ **C. raisins** and/or ½ **C. chopped walnuts.**

1 muffin of 10 *(approx. $.15)*
   Exchanges: 0.25 milk, 1.5 bread; 171 calories, 5 grams protein (10%), 4 grams fat (18%), 22 mg. cholesterol, 38 grams carbohydrate (72%), 5 grams dietary fiber, 174 mg. sodium

❧ BAKED BROWN BREAD ❧

1 Medium Loaf or 2 Mini-Loaves

Especially tasty with raisins. For best slicing, make a day ahead and slice next day. Freezes well. Why not double or triple the recipe and make extra loaves to freeze?

Bake: 350° for 50-60 minutes, uncovered (8½" x 4½" loaf pan)

1. In a small bowl cover with hot water and let stand to soften:

   ¾ C. raisins, optional

2. In a large mixing bowl whisk molasses and soda together:

   ¼ C. molasses (blackstrap preferred)   **½ tsp. baking soda**

3. Whisk into molasses mixture:

   2 eggs   **1⅓ C. buttermilk (or yogurt thinned to**
   ½ C. crystalline fructose *(p. 163)*   **same consistency)**
   or honey

4. In separate bowl, blend flour and salt; fold into liquid ingredients:

   3 C. whole wheat pastry flour *(p. 163)*   **1 C. chopped walnuts, optional**
   ½ tsp. salt   **1 C. raisins, well-drained**

5. Pour into well-sprayed pan; bake until knife comes clean from center. Remove from pan and cool thoroughly before slicing.

VARIATION: In place of 1 C. wheat flour use **¾ C. cornmeal, ¼ C. rye flour.**

1 slice (16 slices per loaf), with raisins, without nuts (approx. $.20), Exchanges: 0.25 meat, 2 bread, 0.5 fruit; 175 calories, 4 grams protein (9%), 1.5 grams fat (8%), 27 mg. cholestrol, 40 grams carbohydrate (83%), 3 grams dietary fiber, 122 mg. sodium

ORANGE MUFFINS

*Flavorful muffins to make using **Quick Muffin Mix**, p. 167.*

Bake: 350° for 20-25 minutes

1. Preheat oven. Spray muffin cups with non-stick spray or line with muffin papers (10 cups for larger muffin pan, 12 for smaller).

2. In large mixing bowl whisk together thoroughly:

   2 eggs
   ¼ C. water
   6 oz. can frozen orange juice, undiluted, thawed

3. Blend mix into liquid ingredients, just until mixed; fold in orange:

   1 bag (2¼ C. plus 1¼ tsp.) *Quick Muffin Mix* *(p. 167)*, **room temperature**
   1 small orange, peeled, chopped

4. Fill muffin cups evenly with batter; fill any empty cups half full of water. Bake until done, about 20-25 minutes. Cool in pan 5 minutes before removing if not using muffin papers.

VARIATION: For more cake-like texture add **2 tbsp. olive oil** *(p. 171)* in step 2.

1 muffin of 10 *(approx. $.20), Exchanges: 0.25 milk, 1.5 bread, 0.75 fruit; 142 calories, 3.5 grams protein (10%), 1 gram fat (8%), 31 mg. cholesterol, 31 grams carbohydrate (82%), 2 grams dietary fiber, 196 mg. sodium*

BUTTER SPREAD

1 Cup

Combine saturated and unsaturated fat for a balanced fat spread! Avoids the hydrogenated fat of margarines. Stays spreadable directly from the refrigerator, but don't leave it out too long or it will return to a semi-liquid.

1. Whisk together, gradually adding oil to butter until smooth and no lumps:

   1 stick (¼ C.) lightly salted butter, very soft
   ½ C. canola or safflower oil

2. Refrigerate in covered container.

1 tbsp. (approx. $.06), Exchanges: 2.5 fat; 110 calories, 12.5 grams fat (100%)

ABOUT THE OILS

CANOLA OIL: High in monounsaturated fat* with best balance of essential fatty acids of commonly available oils: 60% monounsaturated, 24% linoleic acid, 10% linolenic acid. Pleasant tasting in *Butter Spread* and provides valuable essential fatty acids; also acceptable for baking. I recommend *Spectrum Naturals* brand from health food stores.

SAFFLOWER OIL: The most polyunsaturated fat,* highest in essential fatty acid: 77% linoleic acid; best for uses where not heated such as salad dressings or *Butter Spread*. I recommend an unrefined brand from health food stores, but it will have a strong flavor.

*High monounsaturated fats (e.g., canola and olive oils) are safer when heated (along with saturated fats such as butter) because they do not break down as easily as polyunsaturated fats into harmful compounds. **Olive oil**, *the highest monounsaturated fat, is the safest oil for baking and long-term storage. Its strong flavor does not come through in baking.*

LEMON GINGER MUFFINS

A deliciously light muffin that complements soups and main dishes using **Quick Muffin Mix,** *p. 167.*

Bake: 375° for 18-20 minutes

1. Preheat oven. Spray muffin cups with non-stick spray (no muffin papers).

2. Blend milk and soda until mixture foams up, about 1 minute:

   1 C. buttermilk   **¹/₂ tsp. baking soda**

3. In large mixing bowl whisk together:

   2 eggs, beaten light   **2 tbsp. olive oil,** *(p. 171)* **optional**
   2 tbsp. grated lemon peel   **(for more cake-like texture)**

4. Blend ginger into mix; blend alternately with buttermilk into liquid ingredients:

   1 bag (2¹/₄ C. plus 1¹/₄ tsp.) Quick Muffin Mix *(p. 167)*, **room temperature**
   1 tsp. powdered ginger

5. Fill muffin cups evenly with batter; fill any empty cups half full of water. Bake until done, about 18-20 minutes. Cool in pan 5 minutes before removing.

6. Blend **¹/₄ C. lemon juice** with **1 tbsp. crystalline fructose** *(p. 163)* or **honey**. Dip tops and bottoms of muffins in juice mixture.

1 muffin of 10, *oil not included (approx. $.15), Exchanges: 0.25 meat, 0.25 milk, 1.5 bread; 169 calories, 5 grams protein (11%), 2 grams fat (11%), 44 mg. cholesterol, 35 grams carbohdyrate (78%), 3 grams dietary fiber, 222 mg. sodium*

HONEY BUTTER SPREAD

Reduce the butterfat by 50% and make it stretch with this tasty treat spread on cornbread, muffins, bread, waffles. Contains ¼ the fat of butter.

Vigorously blend honey into butter with a wire whisk until smooth:

¼ C. lightly salted whipped butter, softened
½ C. honey (of pourable consistency; warm slightly if needed)

1 tbsp. *(approx. $.06), Exchanges: 0.5 fat; 70 calories, 3 grams fat (38%), 8 mg. cholesterol, 11.5 grams carbohydrate (62%), 32 mg. sodium*

TANGY SPREAD

You'll love this alternative to butter on breads! Less than half the fat of butter.

Vigorously blend together equal amounts of the following until smooth and no lumps remain:

softened butter
nonfat plain yogurt
light cream cheese or cream cheese

1 tbsp. *(approx. $.11), Exchanges: 1 fat; 49 calories, 5 grams fat (92%), 14 mg. cholesterol, 61 mg. sodium*

PUMPKIN GEM MUFFINS

10-12 Muffins

A tasty muffin with a little spice using **Quick Muffin Mix***, p. 167.*

Bake: 350° for 20-25 minutes

1. Preheat oven. Spray muffin cups with non-stick spray or line with muffin papers (10 cups for larger muffin pan, 12 for smaller).

2. In large mixing bowl whisk together thoroughly:

   1 egg   **1 C. pumpkin (canned, cooked)**
   2 tbsp. olive oil *(p. 171)*   **½ C. water**

3. Blend together and mix into liquid ingredients, just until mixed (do not overmix):

   1 bag (2¼ C. plus 1¼ tsp.) *Quick Muffin Mix* *(p. 167)*, **room temperature**
   1½ tsp. cinnamon
   1½ tsp. nutmeg

4. Fill muffin cups evenly with batter; fill any empty cups half full of water. Bake until done, about 20-25 minutes. Cool in pan 5 minutes before removing if not using muffin papers.

VARIATION: Fold in **½ C. raisins** and/or **½ C. chopped walnuts**.

1 muffin of 10 *(approx. $.20)*
   Exchanges: 0.75 fat, 1.5 bread; 181 calories, 3.5 grams protein (8%), 4 grams fat (19%), 21 mg. cholesterol, 36 grams carbohydrate (74%), 3.5 grams dietary fiber, 158 grams sodium

S-o-o-o good over salads and soups! These may be easily frozen in freezer bags. Keep handy to remove desired amount from the bag.

Oven Toast: 300° for 20-30 minutes, uncovered

1. Mix together thoroughly in large mixing bowl:

   1¹/₂ lb. loaf bread, whole grain, cut in cubes *(p. 164)*
   (stack 3 or 4 slices at once to cut in cubes with serrated bread knife)
   1 stick (¹/₂ C.) lightly salted butter, melted
   ¹/₈ tsp. garlic powder or 1 clove minced (mix with butter)
   Spike seasoning *(p. 5)***, to taste, or 1 tsp. sweet basil leaves**

2. Place in single layer on cookie sheet; toast in oven until crisp, about 20-30 minutes; stir and rearrange, if needed, for even toasting.

¹/₂ C. serving *(approx. $.06)*
   Exchanges: 0.5 fat, 0.5 bread; 51 calories, 1.5 grams protein (11%), 2.5 grams fat (39%), 5 mg. cholesterol, 6.5 grams carbohydrate (50%), 1.5 grams dietary fiber, 97 mg. sodium

*Flavorful muffins to make using **Quick Muffin Mix**, p. 167.*

Bake: 350° for 20-25 minutes

1. Preheat oven. Spray muffin cups with non-stick spray or line with muffin papers (10 cups for larger muffin pan, 12 for smaller).

2. In large mixing bowl whisk together thoroughly:

   2 eggs   **2 tbsp. olive oil** *(p. 171)*, **optional**
   1 C. buttermilk   **(for more cake-like texture)**

3. Blend mix into liquid ingredients, just until mixed; fold in blueberries:

   1 bag (2¼ C. plus 1¼ tsp.) *Quick Muffin Mix* *(p. 167)*, **room temperature**
   1 C. fresh or frozen blueberries

4. Fill muffin cups evenly with batter; fill any empty cups half full of water. Bake until done, about 20-25 minutes. Cool in pan 5 minutes before removing if not using muffin papers.

VARIATION: In place of buttermilk use **1 C. yogurt** (thinned to buttermilk consistency) or **1 C. sour milk.**

1 muffin of 10 (approx. $.20), Exchanges: 0.25 meat, 1.75 bread, 0.25 fruit; 145 calories, 4 grams protein (11%), 1.5 grams fat (10%), 37 mg. cholesterol, 31 grams carbohydrate (79%), 3 grams dietary fiber, 236 mg. sodium

SHOPPER'S GUIDE TO...
CORNMEAL, TORTILLAS, CHIPS

YOUR LOCAL HEALTH FOOD STORE IS THE BEST PLACE TO FIND THESE!

CORNMEAL: Stoneground cornmeal includes the whole kernel, containing the valuable germ. Buy stoneground cornmeal or whole dry corn to make your own. In a good blender, whole dry corn can be ground to a coarse meal. It may also be ground in a flour mill.

TORTILLAS: Corn tortillas are best made of stoneground cornmeal, water, salt, lime. For whole wheat tortillas, see p. 164.

CHIPS: The tastiest, nutritionally best corn chips available are made of stoneground cornmeal, canola oil, not hydrogenated or partially hydrogenated (see p. 171), and reduced salt (25% - 40% lower than typical corn chips). For nutritionally best, but not tastiest, buy unsalted stoneground corn chips. In addition, you can buy chips baked without oil (these have more of a hard crunch than the fried chips).

*Cornbread is a perfect complement in flavor and nutrition to beans. Use **Cornbread Mix**, p. 179, with this recipe.*

Bake: 350° for 25-30 minutes

1. Preheat oven. Spray baking pan with non-stick spray.

2. In large mixing bowl whisk together thoroughly:

   2 eggs, beaten lightly
   2 tbsp. unsalted butter, melted
   2 tbsp. canola or olive oil *(p. 171)*
   1 C. buttermilk (or yogurt thinned to buttermilk consistency)

3. Blend mix into liquid ingredients, just until mixed:

   1 bag (2¹/₄ C. plus scant 1 tbsp.) *Cornbread Mix* (p. 179), room temperature

4. Pour into pan and bake until knife comes clean out of center.

5. Delicious served hot with *Honey Butter*, p. 173.

1 piece of 16 *(approx. $.10)*
   Exchanges: 1 bread, 0.75 fat; 116 calories, 3 grams protein (9%), 4.5 grams fat (35%), 31 mg. cholesterol, 17 grams carbohydrate (56%), 2 grams dietary fiber, 180 mg. sodium

CORNBREAD MIX

Enjoy quick cornbread (p. 178) with this home-prepared ready mix! See pp. 163, 165, 177 for information on using mixes and purchasing ingredients.

1. Blend together thoroughly, sifting or stirring through a large strainer to break up any lumps:

   4 C. stoneground cornmeal *(p. 177)*
   4 C. whole wheat pastry flour*
      or 4 more C. cornmeal
   1 C. crystalline fructose
   3 tbsp. baking powder
   2 tsp. baking soda
   4 tsp. salt

2. Store in tightly covered container in refrigerator or freezer up to 1 month. If desired evenly divide mix into **four 6$\frac{1}{2}$" x 5$\frac{7}{8}$" freezer bags.** Each will make **one 8" or 9" bake pan.** In each bag place:

   2$\frac{1}{4}$ C. plus scant 1 tbsp.

   Timesaver Tip: *For quick reference write page number of cornbread recipe on packages (p. 178).*

3. Important to the rising: Bring mix to *room temperature* before using.

*Kamut flour (p. 163) may be substituted.

*Add a final touch of homeyness to your meal with these tender biscuits using the **Buttermilk Biscuit Mix**, p. 181. See pp. 72, 163, 165 for information on using mixes and purchasing ingredients.*

Bake: 400° for 10-15 minutes

1. Blend egg with water or buttermilk; stir in mix just until evenly moistened:

    1 egg, beaten
    ³/₄ C. water (for mix containing powdered buttermilk only)
        or ³/₄ C. buttermilk
    1 bag *Buttermilk Biscuit Mix* (p. 181)**, room temperature**

2. Drop dough in large spoonfuls on ungreased cookie sheet, allowing a little room between biscuits.

3. Bake until lightly browned. Serve hot.

VARIATION: Knead dough about 10 times on lightly floured board or pastry sheet. Pat dough out about ³/₄" thick. Cut with floured cookie cutter or rim of a glass.

1 biscuit of 12, using fresh 2% fat buttermilk (approx. $.15)
    Exchanges: 1.5 bread, 0.75 fat; 153 calories, 4 grams protein (10%), 5 grams fat (28%), 27 mg. cholesterol, 25 grams carbohydrate (62%), 3 grams dietary fiber, 142 mg. sodium

*Ready mix for jiffy **Drop Biscuits,** p. 180. See pp. 163 and 165 for information on using mixes and purchasing ingredients.*

1. Blend together dry ingredients thoroughly, sifting or stirring through a large strainer to break up any lumps; cut lightly salted butter in with pastry blender or two table knives until crumbly (the size of small peas):

10 C. whole wheat pastry flour*	**2 tsp. baking soda**
³/₄ C. powdered buttermilk, optional *(p. 72)*	**2 tsp. salt**
(see variation below)	**2 sticks (1 C.) butter,**
¹/₄ C. baking powder	**cold (but not hard)**

2. Store in tightly covered container in refrigerator or freezer up to 1 month. If desired evenly divide mix into **four 6¹/₂" x 5⁷/₈" freezer bags**. Each bag will make approximately **1 dozen biscuits**. In each bag place:

   2³/₄ - 3 C.

   Timesaver Tip: *For quick reference write page number of biscuit recipe on packages (p. 180).*

3. Important to the rising: Bring mix to *room temperature* before using.

VARIATION: Powdered buttermilk is sometimes hard to find *(see p. 72)*. It may be omitted and fresh buttermilk used in the recipe *(p.180)* in place of the water.

*Kamut or spelt flour may be substituted. When using spelt, reduce the liquid called for in recipe to ¹/₂ C.

This elegant fruit dessert takes 10 minutes or less to prepare. Toast the coconut while cutting up the fruit.

Mix together; chill before serving:

> **1 medium orange (peeled, cut into chunks)**
> **1 C. pineapple chunks, fresh or canned unsweetened**
> **2 tbsp. raisins**
> **2 tbsp. toasted unsweetened coconut***
> **1 tsp. crystalline fructose** *(p. 163)*

*Available at health food stores in macaroon, medium, and coarse shred; I use medium shred in this recipe. To toast, place on cookie sheet in 325° oven for about 8 minutes, watching closely as it browns very quickly.

VARIATIONS: Coconut may be untoasted, but the toasting adds something special to this dessert. Add **sliced bananas.** Add in place of, or in addition to, pineapple **½ mango** (peeled, cut into chunks).

1 serving of 2 *(approx. $.25)*
    Exchanges: 0.5 fat, 1.5 fruit; 130 calories, 1.5 grams protein (4%), 3 grams fat (19%), 27 grams carbohydrate (77%), 4 grams dietary fiber, 3 mg. sodium

Meal Planning Made Easy

PLAN #1   Use the menu plans given with each *Meals in Minutes* main dish.

PLAN #2   Follow these steps to plan dinner meals:

1. Choose the main dishes for a week or for a month using *Main Dish Menu Planning*, p. 185.

2. Plan the remainder of each dinner meal for the week using *Completing the Menu Chart*, p. 189.

3. Consider *Tips for Appetizing Menus*, p. 191, for contrast in colors, textures, shapes, temperatures, and flavors.

4. Follow the suggestions for *Adjusting the Fat Level of Menus*, p. 193.

Colorful, juicy, and refreshing! A "5-minute" dessert.

1. Chill the juices in advance.

2. Blend the juices; divide the sherbert into dessert dishes and pour the juice over it in amount desired:

   12 oz. can apricot nectar
   12 oz. can unsweetened pineapple juice
   6 oz. can grapefruit juice
   2 pts. (1 qt.) lemon or pineapple sherbet

3. Serve immediately.

1 serving of 8 *(approx. $.45)*
   Exchanges: 1 fruit; 146 calories, 36 grams carbohydrate (98%)

Main Dish Menu Planning

*F*ollow these steps for the easiest main dish menu planning ever!

1. Decide what *type* of main dish to serve each day of the week, for example: fish dish on Mondays, bean dish on Tuesdays, etc. (see sample *Main Dish Menu Plan*, p. 187).

   If you particularly like or have more recipes for a certain type dish, you might have more than one day with the same type.

2. Write these dish types at the top of your weekly or monthly menu chart in the appropriate day columns.

3. Use the listing of the different types of dishes in the *Index* plus your own prepared list of recipes by types to choose the weekly or monthly main dishes for your menu.

LITE CHOCOLATE PUDDING

3 Cups ~ Serves 6

It's okay to be a chocolate lover, occasionally! Done in 10 minutes and plenty rich.

1. In a medium or quart saucepan stir together well:

   ¹/₂ C. crystalline fructose *(p. 163)*
   6 tbsp. unsweetened cocoa powder

2. In a 1 quart measure whisk cornstarch into milk until well blended:

   3 C. nonfat (skim) milk
   3¹/₂ tbsp. cornstarch

3. Gradually whisk milk and cornstarch into cocoa mixture. Bring to a boil over medium-high heat, stirring constantly. Continue cooking at low boil for 2 minutes while stirring. Remove from heat.

4. Stir in:

   1 tsp. vanilla
   dash salt

5. Pour into dessert dishes and chill in refrigerator.

1 serving of 6 (about ¹/₂ C.) *(approx. $.25)*
   Exchanges: 0.5 milk, 0.5 bread, 0.25 fat; 148 calories, 10 g. protein (27%), 1 gram fat (6%), 3 mg. cholesterol, 25 grams carbohydrate (68%), 12 mg. sodium

✿✿✿ SAMPLE MAIN DISH MENU PLAN ✿✿✿

SUN.	MON.	TUES.	WED.	THURS.	FRI.	SAT.
Leftovers/ Misc./Soup	**Fish**	**Bean**	**Gr. Turkey**	**Cheese**	**Chicken**	**Veg./Grain**
Leftovers or *Crockpot Garden Soup* (p. 108)	*Tuna Fettucini* (p. 18)	*Crockpot O' Limas* (p. 106)	*Sweet 'n Sour Beans* (p. 14)	*Naturally Nachos* (p. 132)	*Chicken Curry* (p. 16)	*Baked Potato Gourmet* (p. 134)
Leftovers or *Navy 'n Green Bean Soup* (p. 110)	*Lemon Baked Fish* (p. 122)	*Best Burrito Beans* (p. 24)	*Tamale Pie* (p. 26)	*In-a-Minute Pizza* (p. 138)	*Chicken Tetrazzini* (p. 28)	*Golden Waffles* (p. 140)
Leftovers or *Barbecue Franks 'n Beans* (p. 90)	*Tuna or Salmon Loaf* (p. 34)	*Chili Gourmet* (p. 86)	*Emilie's Noodle Bake* (p. 36)	*Macaroni 'n Cheese* (p. 88)	*Chicken Hawaiian* (p. 38)	*Baked Yams* (p. 130)
Leftovers or *Chicken Soup* (p. 76)	*Tuna Bunsteads* (p. 116)	*Black Beans* (p. 45) *and Mexican Rice* (p. 46)	*Sweet 'n Sour Meatballs* (p. 50)	*Broccoli Rice Casserole* (p. 80)	*Chicken Pot Pie* (p. 48)	*Lentil Rice Casserole* (p. 56)

9" Pie Pan or 8-9" Square Pan ~ Serves 8-9

A light dessert and one of our most often served for company! Cut 8 servings from pie pan or 9 servings from square pan. Garnish, if desired, with strawberry halves and/or kiwi slices.

1. **Graham Cracker Crust:** Blend crumbs, fructose, and butter thoroughly with a fork; pat into bottom of 8" or 9" square pan or in bottom and sides of pie pan; chill in freezer 10 minutes or longer:

1 C. whole wheat graham cracker crumbs* (1 packet of 6 crackers)	**1 tbsp. fructose** *(p. 163)* **¼ C. melted unsalted butter**

2. Whisk gelatin into juice in small saucepan; let stand 5 minutes to soften; over medium low heat, bring to a boil, whisking constantly to dissolve gelatin; remove from heat and blend in honey:

about ⅓ C. pineapple juice (drained from 8 oz. can crushed pineapple)	**2 packages (4 tsp.) unflavored gelatin** **¼ C. honey**

3. In mixing bowl whisk together thoroughly, pour into chilled crust, and refrigerate until set:

3 C. lowfat or nonfat plain yogurt **dissolved gelatin and juice**	**crushed pineapple (from 8 oz. can)** **1½ tsp. vanilla**

I use **Mi-Del 100% Honey Grahams (whole wheat), available at health food stores.*

1 serving of 9 *(approx. $.40), Exchanges: 0.75 milk, 0.75 bread, 0.5 fat, 0.25 fruit; 203 calories, 6.5 grams protein (13%), 4.5 grams fat (20%), 12 mg. cholesterol, 34 grams carbohydrate (67%), 1 gram dietary fiber, 141 mg. sodium*

✧✧✧ COMPLETING THE MENU CHART ✧✧✧

STARCH	VEGETABLE	SALAD	BREAD	DESSERT**
brown rice	dark leafy greens	tossed	muffins	fresh fruit
beans	broccoli	cabbage	cornbread	*Yogurt Pie*
potatoes	green peas	orange-lettuce-banana	biscuits	*Orange Ambrosia*
pasta	corn	carrot-raisin	baked brown bread	*No-Bake Cookies*
	green beans	gelatin	sourdough bread	*Lite Chocolate Pudding*
	carrots	arranged	tortillas	*Alice's Fruit Soup*
	cabbage	Waldorf	hot rolls	*Fruit Shrub*
	zucchini			*Chocolate or Carob Blancmange*
	tomatoes			
	squash			**Choose occasionally.
	beets			

189

A simply delectable pudding! Make with carob or chocolate. A good recipe to introduce carob.

1. In medium saucepan or double boiler add chocolate (or carob blended with water until smooth) to the milk; heat until hot, but not boiling:

   1½ C. lowfat milk
   1 oz. square unsweetened chocolate
   **   or 3 tbsp. carob powder plus 2 tbsp. hot water**
   **   (stir carob through a strainer to remove any lumps)**

2. Meanwhile, in a measuring cup whisk gelatin into cold milk; let stand 5 minutes to soften:

   ½ C. cold lowfat milk   1½ packages (3 tsp.) unflavored gelatin

3. Stir softened gelatin into hot milk mixture; continue to stir with whisk until gelatin is dissolved, about 1 minute. Remove from heat; whisk in:

   ¼ C. honey or ⅓ C. crystalline fructose *(p. 163)*
   1 tsp. vanilla

4. Pour into mixing bowl and chill in refrigerator until partially set; fold in:

   ½ pt. whipping cream, whipped (2 C. whipped)

5. Fill dessert dishes or serving bowl; return to refrigerator until set.

1 serving of 8 (about ½ C.) with carob (approx. $.25), Exchanges: 0.25 milk, 2.25 fat; 180 calories, 4 grams protein (8%), 12 grams fat (59%), 45 mg. cholesterol, 15 grams carbohydrate (33%), 43 mg. sodium

Tips for Appetizing Menus

1. Variety in **COLORS** (e.g., 3 different colors)

2. Variety in **TEXTURES** (e.g., some soft, some crisp)

3. Variety in **SHAPES** (e.g., some long, some round)

4. Variety in **TEMPERATURES** (e.g., some hot, some cold)

5. Variety in **FLAVORS** (e.g., complement strong with mild)

2 Dozen

These rich little cookies are fun to make in a jiffy, and the fat content is not out of sight at 29%. But eat only one—for a treat!

1. In a medium saucepan whisk milk, water, and carob powder together; add chocolate and butter; heat on low until chocolate and butter melt:

   ½ C. nonfat milk   **1 oz. square unsweetened chocolate**
   2 tbsp. water   **½ stick (¼ C.) unsalted butter**
   3 tbsp. carob powder
   (stir through strainer to remove lumps)

2. Bring to a boil and boil 1 minute. Remove from heat and whisk in:

   ½ C. honey   **1 tsp. vanilla**

3. Blend dry ingredients thoroughly; stir into cooked mixture with large spoon:

   3 C. raw rolled oats (old fashioned or quick)
   ¼ C. non-instant, nonfat dry milk powder,* optional

4. Drop by spoonfuls on cookie sheet lined with wax paper. Chill until firm.

*Purchase at health food stores.

***1 cookie of 2 dozen**, includes milk powder (approx. $.10), Exchanges: 0.75 bread, 0.5 fat; 94 calories, 2.5 grams protein (11%), 3 grams fat (29%), 6 mg. cholesterol, 15 grams carbohydrate (60%), 1 gram dietary fiber, 8 mg. sodium*

VARIATIONS: Add **½ C. peanut butter** before oats; add **½ C. chopped nuts** and/or **½ -1 C. unsweetened coconut.** For carob cookies, omit chocolate; increase to **⅓ C. carob.** For chocolate cookies, omit carob; increase to **2 squares chocolate.**

ADJUSTING THE FAT LEVEL OF MENUS

The key to controlling fat is not a recipe alone, but *what's on the menu*.

For example, while *Chicken Curry* is 36% fat, the *Chicken Curry Menu* contains only 20% fat (p. 16). And *Tuna Fettucini* is high at 45% fat, but the *Tuna Fettucini Menu* is a more acceptable 26% fat (p. 18).

Meals in Minutes average 26% fat, but if you wish to reduce the fat even further:

- Choose a lowfat, non-oil-based salad dressing.

- Omit or reduce high-fat spread for bread; serve plain or with all-fruit or low-sugar jam.

- Use fat-free sour cream, nonfat yogurt and milk.

- Reduce the portion of higher fat main dish and increase lower fat menu items.

- Reduce amount of cheese or meat in recipe and increase the vegetables.

- Use reduced-fat cheddar cheese.

- Use the lowest fat ground turkey available—up to 99% fat-free.

- Serve the *Vegetarian Alternative* for the main dish.

A Biblical View of Food...

1. Food was the Creator's first gift.

   Then God said, "I give you every seed-bearing plant on the face of the whole earth and every tree that has fruit with seed in it. They will be yours for food" *(Genesis 1:29).*

2. The management mandate for human responsibility includes growing and preparing food.

   God blessed them and said to them, "Be fruitful and increase in number; fill the earth and subdue it. Rule over the fish of the sea and the birds of the air and over every living creature that moves on the ground" *(Genesis 1:28).*

3. Food is the focus of the human declaration of independence.

   When the woman saw that the fruit of the tree was good for food and pleasing to the eye, and also desirable for gaining wisdom, she took some and ate it. She also gave some to her husband, who was with her, and he ate it *(Genesis 3:6).*

194

4. The Creator demonstrated human dependence with a hand-to-mouth supply of food.

> *He humbled you, causing you to hunger and then feeding you with manna, which neither you nor your fathers had known, to teach you that man does not live on bread alone but on every word that comes from the mouth of the LORD* (Deuteronomy 8:3).

5. Jesus, the Bread of Life, satisfies every human need.

> *Then Jesus declared, "I am the bread of life. He who comes to me will never go hungry, and he who believes in me will never be thirsty"* (John 6:35).

6. Food choices are not the test of relationships. Freedom of choice (as opposed to license or legalism) with sensitivity to others is the guideline.

> *The man who eats everything must not look down on him who does not, and the man who does not eat everything must not condemn the man who does, for God has accepted him . . . . He who eats meat, eats to the Lord, for he gives thanks to God; and he who abstains, does so to the Lord, and gives thanks to God* (Romans 14:3,6).

I love working with food. I marvel at the variety, the textures, the flavors, the colors, and the endless ways to prepare it. I like nothing better than to serve others a beautiful, satisfying meal of tasty, nutritious food. I had this interest even before I began a college career in home economics education.

But I had little awareness of the Master Chef, the personal Creator who had originated the foods I loved to prepare. My background wasn't religious, although from childhood I believed in my own idea of God. I had heard of Jesus, but I understood Him only as the greatest man who ever lived. I thought He was not essential to my belief in God. And while my belief in God was a security, I had but a vague understanding of who He really was.

When I began to attend a Bible study in my dormitory during college (under the pressure of much friendly persuasion), I brought my own idea of Jesus—the greatest man who ever lived—to the study. And that was all. I wasn't aware that He had created a complete meal for more than 5,000 people out of 2 fish and 5 loaves of barley bread by just saying the word! I soon learned that my conception of Him was far too limited.

> *In the beginning was the Word, and the Word was with God, and the Word was God . . . . The Word became flesh and made his dwelling among us. We have seen his glory, the glory of the One and Only, who came from the Father, full of grace and truth* (John 1:1,14).

Who was Jesus Christ? The greatest man who ever lived? Yes! But much more. He was the living God. Was it possible that I could believe in God and reject Jesus Christ? No! **Through him all things were made; without him nothing was made that has been made** (John 1:3). Jesus Christ was present and active in the creation of the world.

Why did I need to concern myself with believing in Jesus Christ? Because He sought a personal relationship with me. **My sheep listen to my voice; I know them, and they follow me** (John 10:27). He created food for me, but He created me for Himself. And He designed me to live in a creature-creator relationship to Himself, to honor and reflect His creative and moral magnificence.

Yet, there is a split between human beings and God which has been widening ever since Eve deliberately chose to defy His instructions. She suffered the consequences of that choice—separation from His fellowship and physical and spiritual death. She chose to make her decisions about life independently of God, and that is exactly what I had done, too.

No one had ever explained to me that I was "spiritually dead" or that the purpose of God the Son becoming flesh was to accept the death penalty, to pay the price for humanity's rebellion, humanity's independence from God, and to restore true fellowship with Him.

Imagine, the eternal, living, personal God taking my death sentence upon Himself! Thus I discovered it is not possible to honor God or to know Him without Jesus. I learned that receiving God the Son, Jesus Christ, was receiving the Father as well. **I am the way and the truth and the life. No one comes to the Father except through me. If you really knew me, you would know my Father as well. From now on, you do know him and have seen him . . . . Anyone who has seen me has seen the Father** (John 14:6-7,9).

I made a personal commitment of my life to Jesus Christ. ***Yet to all who received him, to those who believed in his name, he gave the right to become children of God*** *(John 1:12)*. It was a new beginning of forever living, not easy living but living the way for which I was created.

Jesus said, "I am the bread of life. He who comes to me will never go hungry . . . . I am the living bread that came down from heaven. If anyone eats of this bread, he will live forever" *(John 6:35,51)*.

Sue Gregg

200

ABOUT SUE GREGG

At age 17 Sue Gregg was invited to supervise food preparation at a church retreat. During her college years she took responsibility for food service for student retreats and international house parties.

For six summers she supervised the feeding of hundreds of junior highers, high schoolers, collegians, and families at a Catalina Island camp 26 miles off the California coast—all without electricity, freezer, or truck delivery. Food was shipped by ocean-going barge. In addition to meeting a budget calculated to pennies, she worked without the convenience of an office or telephone. The camp goat once invaded her cabin and ate two weeks of menu plans and a mail-order grocery list!

After baby number four and a family health crisis, Sue Gregg began to question how to put nutritional value back into Betty Crocker-style family meals. Nine months on a rigorous, restrictive "health-food" diet convinced her that few families would survive drastic dietary changes, although she experienced positive results.

209

That motivated Sue to experiment with old family recipes to see if it would be possible to retain familiar tastes and textures with optimal nutritional quality. Soon others began requesting recipes and cooking classes. That launched Sue into cookbook writing. With her husband, Rich, she continues writing the *Eating Better Cookbook* series. The couple conduct seminars nationwide and are available for radio interviews and television cooking demonstrations.

COOKING SEMINARS

Spend an hour with Sue Gregg and your whole life at the supermarket and in the kitchen will change. Discover her secrets to eating better and pleasing family palates. In an *Eating Right! Seminar,* participants benefit by learning how to enhance both nutritional value and appetite appeal. At the same time they discover how Sue's simple menu planning system saves time and money. In addition Sue shows how to involve children in the learning process. She believes that healthy eating attitudes are modeled more by "doing" in the kitchen than by academic study.

Eating Right! Seminars apply biblical principles in evaluating commercial foods, popular diet trends, and New Age influences upon the health-food industry. These seminars offer acceptable alternatives aimed at turning yucks into yums.

For information on Sue Gregg's books, cooking courses, seminars, *Sue's Kitchen Magic Seasoning*, or home grain mills write:
Sue Gregg
8830 Glencoe Drive
Riverside, CA 92503
Enclose two first-class stamps.

ABOUT EMILIE BARNES

Energy, encouragement, and enthusiasm are what you get when you spend an hour with Emilie Barnes. Spend all morning with her and your home will be transformed. Spend all day with her and your whole life will be changed.

Emilie practices what she preaches and reaches those she teaches. She captivates audiences and wins friends wherever she goes. The reality of her life gives encouragement that you too can find more hours in your day.

More Hours in My Day is the cry of homemakers and working women everywhere, and the title of Emilie's first book. Emilie married her husband, Bob, while she was a senior in high school. Three years later their first child was born and in six months Emilie was given her brother's three children to care for full-time. As if that wasn't enough, the next year their second child was born. Emilie had five children under five and desperately needed more hours in her day!

As Emilie got herself organized, she found time for herself, her husband, and her

211

God. As a busy woman she survived. And out of her experience was born the ministry of *More Hours in My Day*.

In addition to *More Hours in My Day*, Emilie has authored *Survival for Busy Women*, *The Creative Home Organizer*, *The 15 Minute Organizer*, *The Holiday Organizer*, *Growing a Great Marriage*, *Things Happen When Women Care*, *The Daily Planner*, *The Spirit of Loveliness*, and *The 15 Minute Money Manager*.

She joined Sue Gregg in writing *Eating Right! A Realistic Approach to a Healthy Lifestyle* to answer questions women repeatedly ask about food and food preparation.

Much of Emilie's ministry is shared through her books, but her impact is even more powerful in person. She travels throughout the United States and Canada, giving women guidance and hope for making their lives the very best.

For more information about Emilie's books or seminars, write:
More Hours in My Day
2838 Rumsey Drive
Riverside, CA 92506
Enclose two first-class stamps.